MW00468563

FLIP

An Unconventional Guide to Becoming a Real Estate Entrepreneur and Building Your Dream Lifestyle

FLIP:
An Unconventional Guide to Becoming a Real Estate
Entrepreneurand Building Your Dream Lifestyle

Copyright © 2014 By Nick Ruiz

All rights reserved; no part of this publication may be reproduced,
stored in a retrieval system, or transmitted in any form or any
means, electronic, mechanical, photocopying, recording, or other-
wise, without the prior written permission of the publishers.

Table of Contents

Intro

**I went completely bankrupt with real estate investing...
How could you get any value from me?**

Here's a story that may cause an interesting reaction out of you
(let's see):

So, I'm 19 years old and I have never made any real money
in any of my business ventures yet. Maybe I earned a few nickels
and dimes, but nothing to speak of.

I know I'm an entrepreneur at heart and I hate being told
what to do by a boss. Can you relate? I'll bet you can.

So, I am up late watching TV and I see an infomercial
about real estate investing with no money down. I didn't have
any money to speak of at the time and I thought it could be
something I could learn. I've heard of other people making
money and investing in real estate, but I didn't know tons about
it. I thought, "What the heck", and I pulled out my credit card
and paid $250 for the course.

I got the course a few weeks later and devoured all of the
books and CDs within days. I was ready to conquer the world.
I pulled out a few strategies that I thought would work and
moved forward.

I looked through my local newspaper (this was 1999-2000) and found an ad that looked interesting. It read something like:

2/2 duplex
Needs work
Motivated seller
$69,000

In the course, words like "needs work" and "motivated seller" were what I was looking for because that means I could possibly get a bargain.

I called the seller and met him at the property. I looked at the property with no real way to gauge how much work the property needed and we just talked for a few minutes about the property. I was really nervous and I thought he was secretly thinking that I was some dumb kid who had no idea what I was doing. I'm sure you can relate to that.

I called him the next day and said that I would give him $77,000 for the property and asked him to credit me $8,000 back for closing costs and some repairs. It allowed me to virtually get into the property with nothing out of my pocket.

I fixed the property, brought in 2 tenants and was making $500/month profit. I borrowed against this property and bought another duplex and was making about the same on that. I was a 21 year old kid making $1,000/month with a passive investment. I really liked this.

Then, less than a year later, I sold the first one and walked away with $22,000. That was the most money I had ever seen! I was then completely hooked on this business. $1,000 per month was one thing, but someone handing me a lump sum check for $22,000, that was something that was amazing.

A few months later I sold the second property and walked away with $35,000. I thought, "Why would anyone work?" This is a no brainer.

Over the next few years, and into my mid-20s, I built a multi-million dollar net worth buying rental properties. I borrowed millions of dollars from banks. I had almost 70 properties and was flying high.

Within that time period I fixed and flipped some homes and I also learned the amazing strategy of wholesaling. This strategy REALLY revolutionized my business and income.

Wholesaling is, without question, the easiest way to get deals under your belt as a newer real estate entrepreneur. You don't need down payments, good credit, proof of funds, lenders, or anything that goes into a more conventional transaction.

You are actually flipping houses that you don't even own and the profits can be HUGE. The profits can range from a few thousand all the way up to tens of thousands per deal.

The things you do to get a deal done are conceptually very simple and I will go over all of them in great detail in this book. In fact, this is the flipping strategy that will be taught in this book.

Anyway, back to the interesting story.

So I was flying high and had the world by the "you know what" (so I thought). I was running a large business with full time employees, multiple construction crews and almost 100 tenants. I was rehabbing and selling houses on top of the rental business and was also aggressively wholesaling.

Then, in 2008, the mortgage crisis emerged and the largest crash since the great depression came. A lot of my property values collapsed and lost 75-90% of their value. Some of my properties were in the inner city and this is where the most value loss happened.

So there I was, with mortgage balances that were 5-7 times of what the house was actually worth, and I was completely upside down on millions of dollars' worth of real estate. The tables had completely turned and I was freaking out.

After holding on as long as I could, this major economic collapse forced me into bankruptcy. I couldn't believe this was happening. I was Nick, the young successful entrepreneur, and now I was belly up?

How could I show my face to everyone I knew?

That was one question of many. "How was I going to support my family?" was another very important question.

I really was depressed and broke in every sense of the word. I was financially broke. I was emotionally broke. This caused stress to pour into all of the other areas of my life.

Let me tell you something my friend, I know where you are right now. I have experienced all ends of the success/failure spectrum. I know what it's like to live so tight that you even have to question one or two dollar purchases. If you are going through financial struggles and aren't quite where you want to be, I know the feeling. Stick with me on this journey and we can take the internal resources that you have (whether you believe you have them or not) and put your stake in the ground.

Back to the story...

By the way, I have been listening to positive and personal development tapes, CDs, and reading books since my mid-teens. I am a firm believer in feeding your mind on a consistent basis with the right stuff. You can't do it once and expect a permanent result.

Let me tell you something else...

When I was in the "eye of the storm" and going through the toughest times within that tough time, it was extremely hard to apply all of that great stuff I have learned from all of the books and tapes.

But wait, I was practically an expert on overcoming failures and adversity, considering all of the education and training I have had. I should have quickly and methodically worked my way out of this mess with all of the knowledge I have gained over the years.

Here's the deal...

The depth of this trial was so severe nothing could have fully prepared me for it. NOTHING!

So how did I bounce back and get out of this deep hole?

After being down and out and thinking negative thought after negative thought, I quickly realized that I needed to take massive action. I had to get my family's finances back on track out of necessity and needing to survive. I didn't just want to start a "side business" flipping and wholesaling real estate and work on it in my spare time. This was an absolute MUST in my life and "not getting results" was simply not an option. I wasn't able to "not get results."

Think about that. Is that the mindset you have for doing this business? Or is this something you are just going to dabble in and "give a try." Guess what...If you give something a try, you *will* fail. The stars don't align for people that just dabble. PERIOD!

So I exhausted all of my existing resources and contacts. Anywhere I thought that there was an ounce of opportunity for a deal, I went at it full force. I pushed and pushed and pushed.

One day when I was "hounding" one of my attorney contacts, he said that one of his clients was trying to get rid of a property. BOOM! When he described it to me, it sounded exactly what I was looking for. It was a property that needed a lot of work and a hoarder used to live there.

I ended up buying the property, rehabbing it, and selling it for a nice profit. Now I was back, but I had to be extremely smart with the money because it was all I had. I invested some money right back into some marketing and got another deal. I wholesaled that one. Then I re-invested some more and the cycle continued. I started to do more and more deals and pretty soon I built a well-oiled flipping machine.

I was back to complete financial independence as a real estate entrepreneur.

The bankruptcy scenario was the absolute best thing that ever happened to me. It made me ten times smarter and sharper. It made me a more decisive person and better entrepreneur. It allowed me to be able to respond to trials and adversity with a much clearer mind and to proceed with intelligence instead of reacting out of fear and pure emotion. When little headaches came up in the business, I simply rose to the occasion and handled the issue quickly and smoothly. I've been stretched to my limits with adversity, which makes any lesser adversities seem almost easy. The bankruptcy truly added multiple "notches" in my belt of inner wisdom and intelligence. I have much more clarity and field of vision.

Listen, I came up from scratch with this business TWICE. Once was from a complete financial deficit. I haven't run into anyone who can actually say that other than me. I say that and I tell you this story because I want you to realize that wherever you are currently, I have been there.

I have been way up, way down, and everywhere in between. I don't care if you've never done a deal before or if you've done some and need some guidance and fine tuning. I know that I can help you and I can also relate to you.

If I was able to do what I did in a down economy with no cash or credit, almost every excuse for not doing this is crushed.

One of my favorite quotes of all times is this: "When the winds change, you have to adjust your sails."

I came up from scratch TWICE with my real estate strategies. This really does prove that wealth is a mindset and not a "lucky time and place" thing. I proved this, personally! Since then, I have helped many others do their first few deals and really put a stake in the ground that is their own.

These are just some broad strokes of my story, if you want to learn more about me and my journey, you can go to: Alpha-HomeFlipping.com.

Why I wrote this book

I wrote this book for a few reasons.

First off, and most important, ENTREPRENEURSHIP IS THE NEW RETIREMENT PLAN. It's the new 401k, social security, or whatever you want to call it. It allows you to create the future that you want instead of depending on crumbs that most likely won't even be there in the end.

Second, I wanted to share my crazy story of how I went from NOTHING to MILLIONS…Then, how the crash of 2008 forced me into bankruptcy and how I bounced back quickly from nothing AGAIN. This was all with real estate entrepreneurship.

By the way, I used the word "entrepreneurship" on purpose, instead of "investing."

The definition of "invest" is:
>   To put (money) to use, by purchase or expenditure, in
>   something offering potential profitable returns, as interest,
>   income, or appreciation in value.

Putting up a bunch of money and hope that it brings some returns down the road doesn't sound that appealing. Let me tell you what does sound appealing and what you are about to learn in this book. You will learn how to find the right "off market" house, find a cash buyer and pocketing a check for thousands of dollars (sometimes tens of thousands), without crossing your fingers and "hoping" you are one of the lucky few that can flip a house for a profit. If you can do that just once (the whole point of this book), you will quickly develop the confidence and clarity that you will need to do it over and over again until you are completely financially independent. Are you with me?

To do great in this business in the short amount of time that you want to do it in, you need to really be an entrepreneur. You have to be able to build rapport with people, be creative, and adapt in certain environments to keep things going, etc... These are traits of an entrepreneur.

This is a real business and the people that treat it as such see fast results. The people that treat it as a passive investment that they get to when they have some free time will be scratching their heads and saying "this stuff doesn't work "...No, it works, you don't. That's the problem.

I don't want you to go through with the old school wealth building with real estate where you buy one rental property at a time and in 30 years you have a nice little nest egg. That strategy is fine and dandy if you have another great business that is paying you well currently and you want some long term investments. But if you want to be self-made and put your stake in the ground now, that isn't going to cut it.

Listen, I'm not the guy to tell you not to buy a latte in the morning and invest it so you can retire comfortably in 45 years.

I get it. You want financial independence soon so you can enjoy all of the things in life before you need a walker. Having that latte in the morning is okay because life is way too short for it not to be. I mean, come on. I want you to take your significant other to that nice restaurant this weekend without thinking twice. I want you to grab that car you've got our eye on with that lease payment that you think is a little too high. I want you to have your cake and eat it too. You need immediate income now. As that income stays consistent, you can work on other real estate strategies for the long term. But for now, I want to get right to the point and that is how to do your first profitable real estate deal.

The rules of creating financial independence are changing rapidly because of the landslide of resources that have rushed into our lives in a very short period of time. When I first started everything was much harder and more time consuming. Now you can get almost all the info you need to do a deal within minutes.

The huge reason I feel so passionate about this book and its concepts is NOT the actual strategies on how to do this. Don't get me wrong, I love the strategies that I've developed over the years because in the right hands, they are pure gold...But, I get a little more excited about the mental shifts that take place once you implement this stuff.

Notice how I said in the "right" hands in the last paragraph? I will explain more about that later, but for now, I will explain exactly what kind of important shift that happens.

There is absolutely no question that the biggest issue with newer real estate entrepreneurs is that they overcomplicate this business and develop "analysis paralysis." Yeah, I'm sure you have heard this expression before but I'm not just going to say, "don't get analysis paralysis" and just keep moving forward. I'm going to actually walk you through the process that will GUARANTEE that you not only overcome it, but turn it into a fast "decision making" machine.

Being decisive is a very important trait for a real estate entrepreneur to develop and I can help you shortcut the learning curve. Yes, learning curve. Making smart decisions consistently is an actual skill that you can easily develop.

So, do you want to know the secret to being a full time home flipper and getting financial independence ASAP? Of course you do…

Here it is:

Doing your first deal!

Yeah, its genius, I know :)

No, but really, let me explain the actual psychology behind this seemingly simple concept.

When you are first pursuing flipping houses as a side business, you are clouded with so many thoughts like:
"How am I going to know what to say to buyers, sellers, etc…?"
"What if I lose everything?"
"How do I find great deals?"
"I'm brand new, how will I ever carve my way into this business when there are probably long time investors that dominate my local market?"
"How do these deals actually work? All the paperwork is so intimidating."
"Are the people I'll be dealing with going to know that I'm new and think I don't know what I'm doing?"

There is so much more. You know the kind of thoughts I'm talking about. They run through your head at night which leads you to doubt that you can even do this business successfully.

You see, one thing I learned in my long and crazy journey as an entrepreneur is that consistent massive action brings clarity, decisiveness, and minimizes doubt. It's like magic. TRUST ME! It works.

When you take the right steps and blaze through all of your defeating thoughts and doubts on a conscious level, soon they will go away and your confidence will skyrocket. CONFI-DENCE! That's the word that will make you go full time and build that life you desire and deserve.

When you do your first profitable deal, your confidence goes way up and doing the next deal seems much easier. Actually it *is* much easier because confidence makes miracles happen in this business (actually in all aspects of life).

The bottom line is this:

Once you do your first profitable deal, most of your tough work is done. From that point, doing more deals and expanding your business, is just a decision away. PERIOD!

One other important reason that I wrote this book that I will mention is that there are NOT a lot of intense requirements to becoming a successful entrepreneur with real estate. Here's what I mean:

- You don't need to try and think up the perfect product or idea.

- You don't have to cross your fingers and hope the world likes and buys it from you.

- You don't have to risk your life savings to develop your idea with no guarantees.

That is more of the classic way to start a business. Here are the benefits of becoming a real estate entrepreneur:

- You don't need to think of some genius idea.

- Your product (the houses) already exists. You just need to learn how to buy them low and sell them high (I'll be teaching you that).

- You don't have to risk large amounts of capital on something and cross your fingers that it will sell.

It truly is one of the greatest business models in the world and it is available to YOU! What are you waiting for?

Ok, now that you have read some of the main reasons I wrote this, let's move on...

FLIP

**An Unconventional Guide to Becoming a Real Estate
Entrepreneur and Building Your Dream Lifestyle**

By Nick Ruiz

Chapter 1

How to Actually be a Real Entrepreneur

I want to make one thing extremely clear to you before you read further and learn how to get your first deal done:

URGENCY is the boss. What exactly do I mean by that? Well, I mean that having a sense of urgency is what will separate you from the 90 some percent of people who read books and attend seminars, etc., who never make a dime. It's a plain fact. Most people who read any "how to" info never make any money or get any results.

The reason this percentage is so high is because the reader lacks a sense of urgency. Without it, you are dead in the water.

What I mean is that you need a very compelling reason why you are doing this. Mine were simple. Remember I created financial independence twice from real estate, so my "why" was slightly different in each scenario.

The first time (in my late teens and early 20s), I hated the idea of waking up and working for someone else and being told what to do so much that I obsessed over figuring out this "real estate thing." I spent hours reading, doing programs, and making friends that were already very successful entrepreneurs. I focused so much on the pain of having to work for someone else for the rest of my life that it was enough fuel to get me going.

Now the second time I made it was after I had filed bankruptcy and lost everything. I have a family to support, so you can imagine how there was some automatic, built in urgency there. We needed survival money and that is what caused me to take massive action.

Everyone teaches and preaches that you have to take massive action to get massive results. That is a very true statement. I decided to break that down even further and let you know that urgency is what needs to come first so you actually take the massive action. Urgency is the core trait that will allow you to overcome whatever obstacles and road-blocks come up in this business (or any business).

In the new economy that we all live in we all have to fend for ourselves financially. The days of your company or the government taking care of you are over. Unless you think of some great idea that tons of people buy from you, real estate entrepreneurship is your best bet.

You don't have to think of a cool idea and hope it works out. The idea of flipping real estate already exists. All you have to do is figure out how to get in and out at the right prices. That's exactly what this book is going to teach you.

I truly believe that many of the core actions of humans are derived from primal parts of our brains. Some call it the "lizard brain." It's the part that goes into "fight or flight" and deals with survival. I'm not going to go deep into this (even though I could and I'm a freak for this kind of stuff), but I will say that people take the most action when they are backed into a corner or forced to do something out of necessity.

We do exactly enough that we feel we *have* to do to maintain the certain level of comfort that we are accustomed to. Most of the time, comfort is the enemy of progress.

The nice thing about my bankruptcy is that it took away *all* comfort, so massive action was necessary to gain some level of comfort back. I couldn't dabble around and work on things when my time permitted. Every waking thought revolved around extreme hustle and taking action like you wouldn't believe. I'm not saying that you need to become a workaholic. I *am* saying that the only way you will get the massive results you want is to take massive action.

I'm sure I'm not telling you something you've never heard before, but I really want you to understand the core of what drives you, and all other people for that matter.

Now, a lot of you reading this aren't going through bankruptcy or anything remotely as severe as that. The trick for you is to get and maintain the urgency you're going to need to make progress in this business.

Urgency is the fuel in your entrepreneurial tank. Since you may not be forced into action I definitely want to repeat that your "why" needs to be extremely compelling and you should have an emotional attachment to it. It is proven that emotion motivates. I'm not big on the whole "put a picture of a Ferrari on the wall and look at it every morning" philosophy. It doesn't really work.

Now that we covered the "fuel" for the tank, let's move forward...

I really want to cover this "entrepreneur thing" really well before we dive into the hard strategies and tactics. This book is as much about how to actually be a successful entrepreneur, in general, as it is about being a successful real estate entrepreneur. Almost all of the mentioned principles in here carry over into any industry and will help you create the success you truly want.

The reason that I was able to come up and create massive success two different times is because of my mindset and the fact that I took action as an entrepreneur. I did NOT proceed as an investor, especially the second time around.

See, I am stressing all of this stuff for a reason. I don't want you to fall into the statistic of how more than 90% of people that consume "how to" info don't ever succeed or make a dime. Most of the time, it has nothing to do with the info. I know I mentioned that earlier, but this book is worthless if you don't really latch on to these important principles that I'm stressing so hard.

Investors take a more passive approach and wait for things to come their way. Investors don't necessarily try to develop the people skills, creative thinking, adapting mindset, etc., that entrepreneurs do.

Entrepreneurs wake up with passion and urgency and invest in themselves constantly. They are constantly developing their mindset and skills so they will always have an edge in whatever they are pursuing.

You need to wake up every day with an action plan that is going to move you one small step closer to your goal. Again, you aren't waiting for your Realtor to send you a good deal.

I want to touch on one more thing also:

Don't EVER say you don't have the time to pursue your dreams as a financially independent entrepreneur. PERIOD! It's not an acceptable excuse. You actually do have the time. The truth is simply that it is not a priority in your life currently. There are people much busier than you accomplishing ten times more than you are, so zip it with the "no time" excuse. I know that may sound harsh, but sugar coating things will not do you justice or create a lasting impact on you (which is exactly what I'm trying to accomplish here).

In fact, what I just said above (about how there are people out there doing way more than you), is the "mind trick" I play on myself to create a little more urgency when I feel like slacking a little. I quickly think about someone that is currently hustling and waking up earlier than me doing way more than me. This motivates me to push harder... (It creates a mental competitive spirit that will make you stretch your limits).

Subchapter – The poison known as "Comfort" and the "Default Cycle"

Here's the deal...

One of the toughest parts of becoming an entrepreneur is the fact that you have to break some patterns and habits that you have developed over many years. This is an extremely hard thing to do and will cause some pain and discomfort.

Being comfortable is the exact reason that you are where you are. You are exactly at the point where things aren't really that bad, but they also are not that great. This is called a comfort zone.

By the way, if you are that person that is currently backed up against the wall and have urgency coming out of your veins, good for you! Yes, you heard me – good for you! You are going to be one of the select few that get actual results.

If you aren't that person, still read on because it breaks down comfort and you will still learn how to not fall into the "default cycle."

You might be getting a steady paycheck and you're not starving. This is comfortable. You might be able to pay your bills and still have a few bucks left over to have fun on the weekends. This is also comfortable. As long as you can sustain these comfort levels, you won't take the action necessary to catapult yourself as an entrepreneur; you will "dabble" with real estate or anything else and then kind of let it fall by the wayside. You will, then, officially be one of the 90 percenters who don't make money from the "how to" info that you learned.

What is this "default cycle" that I mentioned earlier?

The default cycle is something that is very dangerous. I have to admit that I was a fallen victim of this multiple times in my life as well.

I'll tell you a quick personal story to illustrate how it works and how you can easily fall victim if you're not careful.

Early on in my real estate career I walked away with some nice sized checks. When I was only 20 and 21 years old I had gotten 2 checks that totaled almost $65,000. That was the most money I had ever seen and it quickly got me comfortable. Before I started doing tons of deals I felt the need to take a little break because I was "doing so well."

Now don't get me wrong, I am definitely a fan of rewarding yourself when you accomplish things, but extending that reward too far can be a dangerous thing. That's what I did. Then it hit me that I was falling victim to the "default cycle" and I didn't even know it. I quickly became urgent and aggressive again, but I learned an extremely valuable lesson that I will teach you quickly.

The default cycle works like this:

Step 1 – You get extreme urgency and take massive action.

Step 2 – You get the results that you really wanted and got really excited.

Step 3 – You reward yourself too heavily and take a break because you've "earned it."

Step 4 – You slowly drift back into the place where you started and were trying to get out of.

Step 5 – Your urgency comes back and you start to take the massive action.

And the cycle continues over and over. Let me tell you – this is not fun and can be very stressful and draining. You are dealing with too many highs and lows that are unnecessary.

Maintaining your urgency and striving to take action outside of your comfort zone will eliminate the default cycle and allow you not to fall into this repetitive rut that will frustrate you to no end.

The problem is that you are constantly heating up and then cooling off and you never really get to the end goal that you pictured. You are riding a wave up and down that never ends. I have definitely had lots of personal experience dealing with this vicious cycle and that's how I originally discovered it. Then I started to pay attention to others and noticed that it was extremely common with most people and I named it "the default cycle."

It's called the default cycle because when you deviate too high or too low from your default comfort level you will either heat up or cool off to get back to the "default." The gradual move back to the default cycle is subtle and you don't always recognize it. This is why I'm a firm believer in having a mentor or coach that has a "zoomed out" look at your big picture and can keep you on track when you naturally will deviate.

Subchapter – Mediocrity Validation – What is it? Are you Part of it?

This is also a common theme that I have personal experience with and have witnessed many others fall victim to as well.

Mediocrity Validation has to do with your peer group. I'm sure you've heard the famous expression – "birds of a feather flock together." That is a very true statement. Getting around the right people is the biggest success "hack" in the world, in my opinion. It is the ultimate shortcut to getting where you want to go. Again, I am a "why" guy and I really wanted to break this thing down to its core.

So, when you are around people that are in places that you are aspiring to be, you begin to make progress by pure osmosis. Now, on the other side of the spectrum, if you're around people that aren't doing the things you want to be doing and going places you want to go, the opposite effect will happen by osmosis. Well, not exactly osmosis…

Let me give you a simple example to illustrate my point about Mediocrity Validation and how powerful, yet subtle, it can actually be…

Let's say that you don't keep a tidy house and it's cluttered and messy. You're okay living that way and it doesn't really bother you. You are completely comfortable with it. Now let's say that your main group of family and friends live in a similar way. These people in your life are subtly validating your actions and behavior when it comes to your housekeeping. It's barely even on a conscious level, but it is happening. When you see your friends' houses, you see that their houses are cluttered and messy and it makes you feel okay about your house and you're comfortable with it. And remember, as long as you're comfortable and your behavior is validated by people that you spend most of your time with, cleaning your house and organizing it is nowhere in your near future. You don't believe there is a need for it. Listen to what comes next…

Now, you go out to a cocktail party and meet a bunch of new people and totally hit it off with them. They invite you over to their houses over the next few weekends for couple's game nights and dinner parties. You notice a similar theme with all of their houses – they are all spotless. I think you already know where I'm going here. I want to really illustrate this in detail so you really know why this works and you can implement this extremely powerful principle in your life.

So now it's your turn to host the dinner party. It is an absolute fact that you are going to feel extremely uncomfortable about your house because you've seen how clean and organized your new friends' houses are. You will feel so uncomfortable about this that you will clean and organize your house. The reason that you're going to clean is because it will bring you back to comfort. PERIOD! It's not because you, all of a sudden, feel like having a clean house. You need to get back to a certain level of comfort that you're used to and you know that having these new "neat and clean" friends over when your house is clean, will get you there. If you have them over with your messy house, your discomfort will be through the roof because you know a messy house is not adequate and doesn't fit into the lifestyle of these new friends. This goes back to very primal behaviors of humans and is a simple example.

As you start to really get close to these new friends and you get together at their houses and yours, your scramble to clean the house on their first visit will turn into more of a long term habit. Keeping a clean house will be part of your lifestyle and it will be automatic.

See, habits are learned, good or bad. And when everyone around you validates them they become more and more engrained and automatic. This is not good if the habits being validated are negative or mediocre.

This is the danger of mediocrity validation...

If you're engaging in negative or mediocre behaviors and everyone around you is as well, you'll never get uncomfortable enough to make a change to become better and make progress to a new level.

I know that example doesn't seem to apply here, but believe me, it does. When you're around movers and shakers, entrepreneurs, and dreamers, you will rise up and automatically start engaging in behaviors that all of these people are, because if you don't, you'll start to feel that discomfort that none of us want to feel. As you spend more time with these action takers your conscious action to make progress will eventually turn into a lifelong habit where you are now one of them, making things happen and growing to heights you never thought possible.

Here's the deal...

Most of the time people only do what is expected of them from their close peers or what their peers expect of themselves (which spills over into your expectations for yourself). This is really important and you may not have noticed this before. If you pay close attention to people around you, their habits, and their immediate peer groups, you will start to see some very consistent patterns and behaviors that are completely congruent to what I have been talking about here.

The easiest way to skyrocket your progress to success is to get a personal coach or mentor. The reason Alcoholics Anonymous is so huge and successful is because of the mentorship. You come in and get a sponsor. This sponsor holds you accountable. Even though you may fall off track here and there they are there to immediately get you back on track so you don't get too far derailed. Make sense?

There are a million examples I can give you about how we act based on the expectations of those close to us. The personal training industry is huge. Many people who hire personal trainers already know the kinds of workouts necessary to lose weight and get fit but they need the firm accountability from their trainer to keep them on track. It's in our DNA to let ourselves down with goals but when a third party is involved we don't want to let them down because that will be painful.

The next best thing to getting a personal mentor or coach is what I talked about earlier – make new friends and form that peer group that is taking all the action that you want to be taking. I won't go on about this forever but this stuff is much more important for your success as an entrepreneur than the actual tactics and strategies that I will lay out for you in this book about the flipping process.

When you have the first part of this book down, the sky is the limit for you as an entrepreneur. Whatever you are pursuing you will be able to make a reality because your entrepreneurial foundation is in place. You will be that special 5-10% who actually gets results from your pursuit.

Get it? If you'd like to engage more about this or any other topic in this book, don't be a stranger. Drop by at AlphaHome-Flipping.com and say hi or leave a comment :-)

Chapter 2

The Simplest Way to Start Flipping From Scratch

Before we actually get into the exact steps to doing your first profitable real estate deal I wanted to tell you the exact type of transaction I'm going to be focusing on in this book. There are multiple ways to make money in real estate and the one you are going to learn here is called wholesaling.

You may have already heard of it...

If you haven't heard of it or know what it is let me sum it up for you: (for those of you who have or have even done deals already, stick around because I'm sure you haven't used all of my psychological strategies with sellers and "under the radar" deal finding techniques).

Wholesaling is the process of flipping a home that you don't own.

Huh? Nick, you lost me...

Hang on, let me explain. You're going to love this. In fact, this strategy is what originally sky-rocketed my income in the early days and I continue to do it this very day.

First, you find a seller that will sell you a house at a discounted price. Then you write a contract for the seller to sign.

Now that property is under contract for the price you agreed upon. You then bring in a buyer to pay more for the property than you have it under contract for, and collect the difference. That is your wholesale profit.

I want to give you a simple example, because if you're anything like me, examples are an easy way to grasp something...

You find a discounted property and write an offer for $65,000.

The seller signs it and you have a binding contract. Great!

Then, you bring in a buyer that will pay you $72,000 for the property.

All 3 of you go to closing and you make the difference as your profit. You just made $7,000 without lifting a hammer or paintbrush.

You can make anywhere from a few thousand dollars up to tens of thousands from one deal.

You don't need cash or credit to do these deals. You don't need banks or lenders. You just need to know the secret sauce of finding the right "off market" deals that you can buy at a deep discount and the right buyers that will come in and pay cash so you can get your healthy paycheck.

Now do see why it is the greatest way to start and complete your first profitable real estate deal?

I'm sure you do...

By the end of this book:

- You will have a full understanding on how to find great "off market" deals on a consistent basis.

- You will know how to find the RIGHT buyers so you can get paid easily.

- You will know how to control the transaction and get to closing quickly and painlessly.

- And many more tricks and strategies so you can quickly go through the steps and get paid.

The main reason your buyers will be lining up to give you their money is because you are going to be presenting them "off market" deals that they don't know about. Without you they never would have run into this deal. That is why there is a healthy profit for you, the wholesaler.

Wholesalers get paid because they solve a seller's problem of not being able to sell their home conventionally and they solve the buyer's problem of not being able to find great "off market" deals. It truly is a win/win situation for all parties.

Just in case you were wondering, your buyers are going to be investors who are landlords or rehabbers that fix and flip properties.

Now, you might be thinking, "Hey Nick, I'm interested in rehabbing and selling properties for bigger profits."

My answer to that is:

Yes, there are a few extra steps, but one thing remains constant – you have to consistently be finding home run "off market" deals to fuel your flipping machine. After a few wholesale deals you will easily be able to move up into this lucrative arena of fixing and flipping. I get into rehabbing and selling more at AlphaHomeFlipping.com.

The great thing about wholesaling is that you will learn how to find these great deals and how real estate transactions work, all while getting paid! You can't beat that.

Now that you are fully aware of the type of deal that is going to put you on the real estate "map", let's proceed with how to do this...

Chapter 3

Setting up the Flipping Factory

Subchapter – How to choose the "money" neighborhoods

Okay, choosing the right neighborhoods where you will make the majority of your money, will not take long to figure out.

There is a spectrum of areas ranging from "war zones" all the way up to extremely high-end multimillion dollar homes.

The areas you need to focus on are pretty easy to quickly identify. They are the areas where the landlords and rehab/flippers are buying.

You may be saying, "Hey Nick, I'm totally new and have no clue where those buyers are buying." Let's get into it...

Landlord/Rental Areas

The areas that the landlords in your area love are the rental areas that are above the total "war zones," first of all. You don't want to have to wear a bulletproof vest to go look at a deal. Now let me just say that I have made a good amount of money wholesaling in the war zones, but it really isn't necessary to do it. You won't feel comfortable going into these areas and I don't blame you.

So you want to look at the areas that are low to middle end rental neighborhoods. They can be blue collar areas or areas that are clean with stable working people. I think you can picture the areas I'm talking about. There are decent cars parked on the street and nice clean yards and local businesses.

Landlords look for these factors in the areas they invest, so you have to as well. The more time you spend focusing on the right neighborhoods up front, the quicker and easier your deals will go when you find them. You will already know which buyers like which areas and deals will be 1-2-3. I'm serious. Setting up the "Flipping Factory" takes a little time, but it is the foundation. Once you're done with this, you will simply plug the deals you find into it and get paid.

"Rehab and Flip" Investor Areas

The best area to focus on for these kinds of buyers is the first time homebuyer neighborhoods. This is a phenomenal place for rehabbers (fix and flip investors) to make tons of money. You are going to be one of their sources for deals.

First time homebuyer neighborhoods are great because of a few reasons.

It is a very affordable price bracket, for one. Also, it has the largest pool of buyers. So that is why fix and flip investors love these areas (including myself). I have been rehabbing homes in these areas for a long time and they sell the quickest because of the reasons I just mentioned.

You, as a wholesaler, are going to focus on this neighborhood very intensely. There is a lot of money to be made in these areas and you will have your rehabber/flipper buyers lining up to buy your great deals that you get ahold of.

Now, can you wholesale in other areas? Yes. You can wholesale farms, commercial properties, land, high end homes, etc., but I am presenting you with the areas that are drop dead easy and have the path of least resistance. Once you are well sea-soned in the business you can branch out into those areas, but for now, you need to stick with the quick and easy stuff.

The bottom line is this – you need to be locating great deals in the areas that cash investors love to invest in. Some will be landlords and some will be rehabbers/flippers.

Another easy method for locating great areas is to go to a local real estate group and talk to some of the investors and see where they are buying. This is another easy way to get some clues on the best areas for you to make your money.

Subchapter – Why you need buyers *first* and how to find them

Okay, so most people might think finding a buyer first is backwards. They think in order to buy low and sell high, you have to find a low price first and then find a buyer to sell high to. That is not the way you want to approach this.

You want to locate and talk to cash buyers/investors *first* so that when your deals start to come, you can quickly connect the right buyer to it and spend very little time putting the deal together.

Your cash buyers are one of two components to your flip-ping factory.

Remember, your cash buyers will love to hear about your "off market" deals. They are sick of fighting over the same MLS properties that every other investor is fighting over. For those of you who don't know what the MLS is:

It is the Multiple Listing Service. It is where all of the homes listed with a Realtor are put for sale. All of the investors you are going to be selling to know about the deals on the MLS. If a great deal comes up, the local investors fight over it like vultures and it usually gets bid up to a price that is not that great anymore. That is why your deals are going to be so valuable to your buyer and they will be "standing by" waiting for your call for the next deal.

With technology, the buyers get an automatic email whenever new deals pop up on the market. They are immediately notified when there is a price reduction or a house comes back on the market.

When I first started in this business, auto email did not exist and it was easier to be the only buyer that knew about a new listing. Those days are over. This is why wholesaling has been extremely lucrative and necessary in the marketplace.

Did I make a good enough case why there is a huge demand and a ton of money to be made by wholesaling? I hope so...

So, how do you find cash buyers?

Finding these buyers is not hard at all and you should be able to find almost all of the buyers you will ever need in a couple of weeks or less, depending on your level of action.

Local ads on classified sites

This is extremely simple and very effective. When I coach students one on one, they are always surprised at how fast they get results with this method.

There is a "trick" to this method though. There is a specific way these ads have to be structured in order to get the response that you want.

You are going to want to focus on Craigslist and Backpage as your main sites to do this on. I know that there are other classified sites but focus on the ones that get all the attention. Craigslist is, by far, the one that needs the main focus.

What you need to do is post a simple ad that talks about a fake house deal. You can even put a photo in the ad. Here is what it should look like:

Title: *3br house near (write an intersection in the area you are focusing on) that needs lots of work*

Price: *$50,000 (make this number a very deeply discounted number...50-60% off after repaired value)*

Body: *This is a 3br house that is in pretty rough shape and has been sitting vacant for almost a year. The roof is leaking in multiple spots. The kitchen cabinets are falling apart and none of the plumbing is currently working. The windows are original. The furnace doesn't work and needs to be replaced. The carpet is stained everywhere because of animals. It will need a cash buyer that is used to rehabbing properties. Please respond with your name and number if you are interested.*

Now, let's break this ad down a little so that you can easily duplicate this and produce similar ads to this with ease any time you want.

First off, you probably noticed that it doesn't sound professional and a bit choppy. The bottom line is that you want this to sound like a real property that needs real work. If the person looking at the ad gets a clue that it sounds fake or like some "fresh out of a seminar" real estate person trying to get buyers, they won't even respond. The details in this ad really do matter.

You want to name a real intersection and a real price that is deeply discounted. You want to go into lots of detail about the actual repairs because, again, it adds another layer of authenticity that makes it sound like a legitimate deal that the investor will definitely be interested in. Remember, you don't want to sound like some hot shot wholesaler who does ten deals a month; you just want to sound like a homeowner trying to get rid of an ugly old house.

I've been using this type of ad for years and it is such an easy and effective way to get as many buyers as you could ever want or need. I've fine-tuned these ads and developed this exact structure for maximum efficiency. Don't deviate from this ad structure and try anything fancy because the work has already been done for you.

Now, the next thing that you need to know about the ad is how often you need to post a variation of this ad.

What you need to do is get clear on the different neighborhoods and pockets in your city that you plan on flipping in. These are the areas that I mentioned earlier called the "money" neighborhoods. Once you do that, you need to place an ad every other day for each of these areas until you get 12-15 buyers (minimum) per area.

The key to remember here is that the ads have to sound completely unique and different so that people think that these are all real deals and not some spammer blasting ads online.

Here is another example of a buyer ad:

Title: Cash Buyer Needed for this 4br House

Price: $65,000 (remember 50-60% off after repaired value to make it very appealing).

Body: This house will not qualify for conventional financing because of some minor foundation damage. The bathroom is not functional and stripped down to the studs. You are going to have to tear down the garage because the walls are caving in. Please respond with your contact info if you are interested in this property.

Now I didn't put my phone number at the end of these two examples on purpose for now, but I want to explain what happens if you do or don't. If you put your number in the ad, you will get calls and may need to deal with these buyers on the spot. If you don't put your number in there and ask them to leave their info, you can call them back on your time and you will feel more prepared. I advise not putting your number in the ads in the beginning until you get a little more comfortable talking to the buyers and get used to some of the questions they might ask you.

When they call, you want to focus on a few key pieces of info that will make flipping deals to them in the future very easy, so you don't have to waste any time and get paid ASAP. Here are the main points that you need to cover:

Can they pay cash?

- Can they handle large remodeling and construction projects?

- What areas do they like to buy in?

- What price ranges do they prefer?

- Do they rehab and keep properties (landlord)?

- Do they rehab and sell?

- Can they close quickly?

Now obviously the conversation may be a little different with each buyer, but these are the pieces of info that are most important. You also need to realize that before you can even get into any of these questions, you'll have to address the fact that these people contacting you are interested in this exact property you posted.

You tell them that the property just sold to another investor because it was such a great deal and that you might have another one really soon nearby. Ask them if they would like you to contact them about it when it comes up. They will most likely say "yes" because, of course, they want to know about another deeply discounted property. Once they confirm that they want you to get in touch with them about this future deal you need to break into a few of the questions mentioned above.

Some people look at this as deceptive because you are advertising a property that doesn't really exist. I don't see it that way at all. You are about to start pawning off GREAT deals to the people that respond to this ad that will result in them making tens or even hundreds of thousands of dollars over the next few years by buying and rehabbing them for huge profits. The fact that you took an action to put them in touch with you is worth a lot to them (even if they don't know it yet). You will be adding a lot of value to this new person and it is a win/win for everyone.

How else can you find quality cash buyers?

Go and Meet Them at Your Local Real Estate Groups

Local real estate groups are all over the country and I'm sure you have one in your area.

This is another extremely easy way to find cash buyers. One thing you have to realize about these meetings is that a lot of times there are some presentations where they pitch you some product or service. That is how a lot of these groups make money. They split the profits of the program/boot camp/course or whatever with the speaker.

The real benefit of going to these meetings is what happens before and after it starts. Meeting the people that attend these meetings and getting to know what exactly they do and what kinds of properties they buy is an extremely valuable resource. I don't care if you are a quiet person who isn't really outgoing, you are going to have to come out of your shell a little and shake some hands. It's okay. Most of these people are extremely friendly and love to talk to new people and share some of their knowledge with someone that is truly receiving it.

One thing for sure about the "veteran real estate investors" at these meetings: They all know a lot and love sharing their knowledge with people that make them feel really smart and are amazed at how much they know. In fact, this is true in all areas of life when you are trying to learn from someone. Everyone has an ego and if you stroke it, you'll be able to get all kinds of valuable information that they usually would never talk about. Say things to them like "wow, that's unbelievable" or "I can't believe you've accomplished all of that." These short little compliments can really pay you back in volumes if you truly are sincere about them. Don't sound cheesy about it or they will stop talking to you and go to the bar for a drink...

So, as you dive into a few conversations at these gatherings, start to ask some of these people the questions that I taught you earlier on. Tell them you are working on a few deeply discounted deals and ask them if they want you call them when they come up. Of course they will want you to call them.

If you implement these two strategies consistently, you are going to have no problem getting all the buyers you need to flip your first deal (and many more after).

There are a few other complicated and, "lots of legwork" ways to find a few more buyers, but it is absolutely unnecessary. I am only here to teach you the path of least resistance to get your first deal done. If I list every possibility for every situation it will do you no good and paralyze you into no action at all. If I give you difficult tasks that are extremely labor intensive and take a lot of time, you'll get discouraged and throw in the towel before the magic happens.

I've seen so much of this in life and I will NOT let it happen to you. A big reason that people tend to not follow through with consistent action with most things is because of all the complicated, time-intensive tasks and processes it takes. My whole deal here is to keep things extremely simple and easy to follow. Nothing here is rocket science, it's "ACTION SCIENCE." I made that up by the way, so if you ever hear that anywhere else, they stole it from me :)

Subchapter – Finding a title/closing company that can facilitate a wholesale deal.

This is an extremely important part of the "flipping factory" that shouldn't take long at all to set up.

You MUST have a title company that can work with the types of transactions that you will be doing. Before we actually get into how to get these title companies on board, I want to explain exactly how these simple deals will work. This is so you can easily explain this stuff to the title company that will close your deals for you.

We (as real estate entrepreneurs) call this type of flipping "wholesaling." Many title companies can't facilitate these kinds of transactions and they DEFINITELY don't know it as "wholesaling." In a second I am going to explain the exact way that these deals are facilitated so you can approach these companies with confidence and explain exactly what you are looking for (in their language).

These little details are often not taught and often frustrate beginners when they are just brushed over and not broken down into detail. This book is designed to cover all of the details and subtleties just like I do with my private coaching students. I see the grin on their faces (on video chat) every time I cover these details, where most courses leave them high and dry.

Here are the different ways that a wholesale deal can be done:

1. Assignment of Contract

This is, by far, the easiest and my favorite way to close wholesale deals. I prefer it over the other methods for sure, but it can't always be done.

The way this simple transaction works is like this:

You write a seller an offer to purchase/contract for the agreed upon price and terms. Then you go out and get your buyer to pay a higher price for the property and they write you an offer to purchase/contract. Once they do this, you can fill out an "assignment of contract" form that describes the terms of the assignment. You should be able to find an assignment of contract at any general legal store.

For the "offer contract", I always use the basic offer contract from my local legal form store from my state. I suggest you do the same. The reason that I recommend this, instead of having a custom offer drawn up for you, is that it puts the seller more at ease. Remember, having the sellers comfortable with you is the key to being able to consistently flip great deals. Most of the time, once we agree on a price, I fill in the blanks of the offer with the seller and explain to them that I use standard offers as opposed to a custom offer where there could be hidden language to favor me, the buyer. They ALWAYS like when I tell them this and it definitely adds a level of comfort for them.

What exactly is an "assignment of contract" form and what does it do? What you are doing is assigning the rights to close on the particular property and the agreed upon terms with the seller to another party and you are getting a fee to do it.

I love to learn from examples and I will give you a simple one right now...

You go out and find a deal and you write an offer for $75,000. Then you bring in a buyer that is willing to pay $81,000. Then you fill out the assignment of contract with an assignment fee of $6,000. Then, you will submit your offer to the seller, along with the assignment form to the title company, and they will get the deal rolling. When you get to closing the buyer's funds will cover your assignment fee and the money owed to the seller. You will never have taken title and there usually will be ZERO closing costs to you, because you are just a "fee" on the closing statement that is paid by the buyer. You get a check cut to you for $6,000 and you stroll out of there with a big grin on your face. How much money or credit did you need to do this deal? ZERO (unless you give an earnest money check to your seller for a small amount like $10 or $20).

So the reason this is the easiest and my favorite is because there are usually no closing costs and you don't have to even sign any closing documents since you are not a buyer or seller in the transaction. The deed will go directly from your seller to your buyer.

Now I mentioned earlier that I can't always do my favorite wholesale transaction (assignment of contract) and here's why:

The seller will know that you are not the actual buyer if they really study the closing statement. When you are dealing with a very motivated seller it is usually not a concern. But, when you are dealing with a picky seller, or one that has an attorney, they could start picking the closing statement apart and wondering why you are not the buyer on the closing statement.

Remember, your buyer is a cash investor that is getting a deal, so they could care less if they know that you are assigning the deal or not. It's the seller that may not understand this and wonder why you are getting a "fee" on the closing statement and someone else is buying it. You are not doing anything wrong or trying to fool anyone. Don't ever worry about being unethical, because you are being extremely fair and helping a seller and a buyer in need. You are giving the seller the price that you contractually agreed upon so they should have zero issues. It's just that once in a while you find sellers that like to complain and get picky and it's not worth the headache with an assignment of contract – and that's why I am about to tell you about my next way of doing a deal that eliminates the possibility for any issues like the ones I just mentioned above.

2. Simultaneous Closing or Double Closing

This is the type of transaction where you are actually taking ownership of the property for a few minutes during the closing. This way, there is a closing statement between you and the seller, and a completely separate transaction and closing statement between you and your buyer.

The nice thing about this transaction is that you are actually buying the property from your seller and selling it to your buyer. This way neither party will have anything they can question because things appear more conventional.

Here is the same dollar amount example that I used before, just with a double closing instead of an assignment fee:

You write an offer to the seller for $75,000. Then you bring in your buyer who writes you an offer for $81,000. You submit both offers to the title company and the deal gets rolling. Now, since you are actually taking ownership of the property for a minute, you will have some closing costs. You will have to pay for title insurance when you sell the property and probably some type of closing fee. There may also be some recording and tax fees. In each deal and state these costs vary but they can range anywhere from a few hundred all the way up to $1500 or so. Most of the time it will be under $1,000 though.

So, in this example, you will make around $5,000 instead of your $6,000 from your assignment version of this deal, so just keep that in mind when you are putting your deals together. Obviously, the assignment profit is ideal, but now you understand why it won't always work that way. Either way, you're making a VERY NICE profit!

Now, there are a couple ways that double closings can be funded:

A. Your buyer's funds would "blanket" the entire transaction and can be used for your purchase and then for their purchase. For example (just using easy numbers): Your buyer would bring in the $81,000. Then $75,000 would go towards paying your seller and the remaining $6,000 would go to you and the deed would go from your seller, to you, and then to your buyer. Remember, those were fake numbers just to show you how it would work. The real numbers will be adjusted for closing costs, tax proration, etc...

B. The next way that these deals may need to be funded are by using transactional funding. This is money that you would borrow for a few hours. You would use these funds to pay your seller and then immediately get paid back when your buyer pays you to buy it. You never actually touch these funds, they are held in an escrow account with the title company. These transactional fund lenders do NOT care if you have good credit because they are not actually taking any risk by lending to you. They will wire the money to the title company's trust account once you have the closing set up with your seller and your buyer. They are simply tying up their money for a few hours knowing that the title company will send them a check once the deal closes. There is usually a cost of a couple thousand dollars for you to use this money. I know it sounds high, but it's simply the cost of doing business and you may need to do it on certain deals.

You may be wondering why the heck you would ever use expensive transactional funding when you can just use the buyer's funds to blanket the whole deal. The answer is that you probably won't need this type of funding much, but there are certain instances where you might have to. You might have a title company who requires you to bring in your own funds. You are going to make sure you find one that doesn't require it. I just wanted you to know about these funds just in case you run into a unique scenario where you temporarily need your own funds to pay off the seller. Make sense?

Ok now that you know the two main types of wholesale transactions and how they work, you are ready to actually find the right title companies that you are going to funnel all of your deals to. I'm letting you know up front that most of the title companies that you call will not be able to facilitate these types of transactions. That's totally fine because all you need is one.

You are going to search for local title companies in your area and just start dialing. You are going to ask to speak to a title agent who handles closings. When you get them on the line, you are going to explain to them the types of real estate deals you are working on.

Before I tell you exactly what you are going to say to the companies, I want to make you aware of something that will, most likely, come up when you call these companies. First off, many of the title companies will be very conventional and not even know what you are talking about. Some of them will tell you that you need a real estate license in order to do this kind of deal (completely untrue...they are just uninformed on these types of unconventional deals). They might even tell you that it's not legal (again, TOTALLY untrue). I'm just giving you a heads up that you may have to call many companies before you find one that will tell you they can do it. The point is, don't give up because after enough calls you'll run into the right companies that will help you achieve your flipping dreams :)

So, In order to make this crystal clear, I'm going to lay out the exact conversation and how it should go:

You: Hello, I'm looking to speak with a title agent in your company.

Them: I am a title agent. How can I help you?

You: The reason that I'm calling is because I am working on a few new real estate deals and I want to know if you guys can help me with closing them.

Them: Tell me what exactly you are looking for.

You: I have a deal where I am a buyer and I have an accepted offer for $75,000. I immediately found a buyer to pay a little more for it and I'm going to assign the rights of the contract to my buyer for the difference. He is willing to pay $81,000 so my assignment fee will be $6,000. Can you guys close this deal?

Okay, from there, they will tell you if they can or can't.

The next thing I'm going to show you is how you should ask them about simultaneous or double closings:

You: Hello, I'm looking to speak with a title agent in your company.

Them: I'm a title agent. How can I help you?

You: I am working on a deal that will require a simultaneous closing or double closing. Have you ever done one of those before?

Them: Yes, we do those.

You: Ok, great. Let me ask you this...I really prefer to do the types of double closings where the buyers funds can blanket the whole deal as opposed to me bringing in my own funds for the first part of the transaction. Can you do that?

Them: Yes we can.

You: Great. I'll be in touch with you guys soon.

Now, there were a few variables in this conversation and I want to show you examples of how the conversation could go, depending on how they answer a few of the initial questions.

You: Do you do simultaneous closings or double closings?

Them: No we don't.

Ok, you know that they can't help you with what you're looking for. Here's the next possible outcome:

You: Do you do simultaneous closings or double closings?

Them: What exactly do you mean? (Believe it or not, some very conventional title companies have never heard of it, but could maybe do it if you explain).

You: I'm working on a deal where I am a buyer and I have an accepted offer of $75,000. I immediately found a buyer that is willing to pay me $81,000 for the property and I accepted their offer. I would like to submit both offers to you and close both transactions within the same closing. I would like my buyer's funds to blanket the whole transaction so I can pay off my seller and walk away with my profit between the two prices. Can you do this?

Them: It sounds like something we will be able to do, sure.

Ok, there is one more variable that I want to go over that we haven't talked about yet. It is when they cannot facilitate the double closing with the buyer's funds blanketing the whole transaction.

Here is how it would go:

You: Can you do the double closings where the buyer's funds blanket the entire transaction?

Them: No, sorry. You need to be able to fund your purchase with your own funds and then you'll get immediately paid with the buyer's funds right after.

Now, that isn't the worst scenario in the world, it just means that you will have to use transactional funding, like we talked about earlier. I really just, more or less, wanted you to know that this answer could come up. You really should just keep calling title companies until you find one that will allow for the buyer's funds to blanket everything.

The bottom line is that you shouldn't have a problem finding the right title companies that will be able to do exactly what you want, as long as you call enough of them. I always tell my students that they really need to find two or three local companies that can do their deals, even though you really will be putting all of your deals through one company, and building a solid relationship with them. It's always nice to have a backup, just in case things change with your first company. Got it?

By the way, I know lots of the stuff I just went over wasn't all that exciting, but it is necessary for your flipping factory to be complete. I know what you're thinking: "Nick, how do I actually find all of these great 'off market' deals that you speak of?" Don't worry; I've got you covered on that in GREAT detail. Just bear with me. I don't like to skip around. There is a necessary sequence that makes all of this super simple and very seamless for the long term. I like minimal headaches in all the business that I'm involved in, so I take a little extra time on the front end of things to make sure that stuff is as easy as possible down the road. Don't you agree?

Chapter 4

How to find GREAT "off market" deals

Here we are...

The moment you've all been waiting for! I'm about to reveal to you the exact strategies that I use to get tons of "off market" deals and consistently make a great living with this beautiful business of real estate entrepreneurship.

Now, before we get into the exact strategies, I really want to make a very clear point here that completely coincides with my mission of being a "real estate entrepreneur" instead of a "real estate investor."

Whenever someone starts a business, whether it's retail, a restaurant, an online store, lemonade stand, or whatever, they have to get the word out that they are in business. Right?!? Without letting people know what you do, you will be standing next to your open sign with tears rolling down your face because you'll be all by yourself. Customers don't just automatically find you once you are open. You have to do this little thing called "MARKETING "... Yes, marketing is the absolute bloodline of every business, including the one that I am teaching you about in this book. This is one of the huge differentiators that can take you from a wannabe real estate investor into a real estate entrepreneurial powerhouse. You are starting a business of flipping and wholesaling homes, so you need to absolutely get yourself out there and be known as soon as possible. 90% of real estate people out there have absolutely no clue about this concept and how to do it properly, which is the reason that you will be able to quickly break into this business and find all those "off market" deals and have your competitors scratching their heads wondering how you did it. They will still be pulling their hair out fighting over the crumbs that are listed on the MLS while you scoop up 'home runs' one by one. Sound good? I hope so…

So, you might be wondering exactly how marketing actually converts into getting the great "off market" deals that I've been ranting and raving about. Well, here's how it all works…

You get your message out there in multiple ways about how you pay cash for homes and buy in "as is" condition. Then what happens is you start to get calls from people who may want to sell and some of them will be motivated to sell quickly and hassle free. The whole key here is to get as many motivated sellers calling you as possible, because the more motivated seller leads you get, the more deals you will close. It's simply a numbers game. You constantly want your phone ringing with as many motivated sellers as possible. The fact is, the more you market yourself, the more calls you will get. There will be tons of calls from sellers who are not that motivated and will be a total waste of time. That's okay, because you are just going to move forward and sort through all of these, until you get to the good motivated ones.

You are a problem solver. That's why you get paid as a flipper. The seller is contacting you because they don't have many options and they can't sell it the conventional way for one reason or the other. Maybe they don't have time to wait. Maybe there is a relocation of their job. Maybe they filed bankruptcy and have to liquidate their assets. People sell their houses at a discount when they are truly motivated. In exchange for the discount, you are able to offer them a quick, hassle free process for selling their home. It's a total win/win scenario.

So now that you understand how this process works you are going to learn how to convert these calls into real deals. You need to embrace the fact that some marketing costs a few bucks and some is completely free and just costs your time. If you weigh out the few bucks it will cost you to get you up and running in this business compared to starting businesses on other industries, it equates to PEANUTS! Yes, that is what the cost is to start up as a real estate entrepreneur.

Entrepreneurs market themselves while investors wait for "opportunities" to come by. Which one do you think makes sense if you want to become financially independent ASAP?

Ok. Now that we covered the foundation behind what I'm about to share with you, let me start to show you the many great ways to get sellers calling you. I just want to mention one more thing here...

There is a very certain and specific way to talk to these sellers that call you and there is a spectrum of motivation that you need to decipher so you are not wasting hours of your life on the phone with deals that are completely dead and not going to be profitable. After I go over all of the ways to get your phone ringing, I will talk to you about all kinds of tactics and strategies to actually talk to and deal with these sellers. A lot of this is psychology, persuasion, and just being a people person. Again, my thesis rings loud and proud! You are an entrepreneur (not an investor) and these skill sets that I mentioned above are traits of an entrepreneur and you will need to learn and adopt this stuff. The great news is that I will cover all of this after the marketing strategies and all of these skills are completely learnable. PERIOD! Some people think you are either born with entrepreneurial skill sets or you're not and I stand extremely firm on the fact that it is all as learnable as any other skill. Got it? Good...I'll discuss that fun stuff in a little bit then.

On to the sweet marketing stuff...

Craigslist Ads

Yes, these can, and do work. The great thing about this form of marketing is that it is free and only costs a little bit of your time to implement. The big key to this strategy (along with all of the others) is consistency. Marketing is NOT a one-time thing that will keep you in business forever. It's kind of like being healthy. You can't eat a spinach salad on Monday and expect it to carry your health for the next few weeks while you eat tons of junk food. Being healthy is a daily habit and marketing is a weekly and monthly habit as well.

I'm going to give you a few examples of simple ads that you are going to place in the "real estate for sale" section and also in the "real estate services" section.

Title: *Will Buy Any House 'As Is'*

Body: *We are local homebuyers that pay cash for homes in (your town). We don't care if there are any repairs/updates/remodeling needed for your home. We will buy it "as is" for CASH without any contingencies or inspections. You will not have to pay thousands of dollars in real estate commissions either. Please call us at xxx-xxxx to have a short conversation to see if we can help you out. There is absolutely NO obligation whatsoever and will only take 5 minutes of your time. Thanks*

Here's another example:

Title: *Sell your House for Cash…Quick Closing*

Body: *If you are thinking of selling your home the easy way without any hassle, please call us. We can close in less than 2 weeks if you want and we don't have any contingencies. You don't need to fix or clean anything. We will take it exactly as it sits. Call us right away at xxx-xxxx.*

Now, I want to be completely transparent and crystal clear about the effectiveness of these ads on craigslist. First of all, consistency is the absolute key to this strategy. You MUST post these ads a few times a week, EVERY WEEK. You can't throw up a few ads and think you can just wait for your phone to ring. It may take months before you even get one phone call. But, if that phone call makes you $10,000, I doubt you'll be complaining about all of the ads you posted that didn't work.

The other thing I want to make clear here is the fact that this is probably the least effective form of marketing in this business. I'm a straight shooter and I'm not here to BS you or fabricate the real truth here. Why do you think it's not that effective? For one, since it's free, everyone else is putting up these ads in your town. Your ideal seller will have plenty of other people's ads that they will go through and they might never get to yours. It's the least effective because it's the absolute lowest barrier to entry. I always teach my students to use this as a supplement to a more effective form of marketing that requires a small budget. We will get into more of that soon.

Another little trick you can do is to scroll through some of the ads from your competition and see what they are saying and if they are consistent. Usually if you see their ads for a few months straight, they are most likely getting some type of leads from this method. Look at what they are saying. Look at how they change up their ads throughout the week. I'm always interested in modeling other people for shortcuts, so take advantage of seeing your competitor's ads and copy them.

Now I want to get into the next form of finding good motivated sellers that is much more effective than the craigslist ads...

Bandit Signs

This is a big step up from the craigslist ads on the effectiveness scale. Bandit signs are those signs you see in the street medians and on the highway ramps that say "we buy houses" or something like that. Believe it or not, they can be extremely effective if done properly and strategically.

When you first start off wholesaling bandit signs are a no-brainer because they are cheap and work pretty well in attracting calls from motivated sellers. Most people who use them don't put a lot of thought into putting them out and don't have any type of strategy behind it.

I want to make a crystal clear point here about bandit signs. They are disposable. What do I mean by that? I mean that they don't last that long. When you put them out, you will only get a few days to a week of exposure. If you're lucky, you maybe can get two weeks. Why? Because you aren't supposed to put them out and it's against most city ordinances. It's kind of like littering. Think about what cities would look like if everyone put out their marketing message all over the medians and freeway ramps. It would look like a freaking mess out there. The city workers, and sometimes police officers, will take your signs down if they see them. One time, I got a call from a police officer that called me with a blocked number and told me that I can't do it anymore. I said "ok" and that was the end of the call. I am going to tell you the strategies to make your signs last the longest so you can get the maximum results out of them.

City workers are off on the weekends, so you need to put your signs out Friday afternoons. You will definitely get the full weekend out of them and hopefully another full week after that. The next common sense tip is that you need to put them out in the busiest and highest traffic areas possible. I recommend to my students that they put out 12-15 signs per weekend. You want to mix up your areas and cover a different area every weekend. You'll start to find out which areas are the most effective and where you are getting the most calls from.

Some people that I coach have told me that they have to get over the embarrassment of getting out of your car and putting the sign in the ground in front of all of the cars passing by. My answer to an excuse like that is this, "stay in your car and stay broke then." It's plain and simple. You're going to have to constantly be expanding your comfort zone if you actually want to be a successful entrepreneur. Remember, I'm the ultimate excuse crusher. I came up from scratch twice, and once was after filing bankruptcy. NO EXCUSES HERE!

If you want to be a little extra slick and get super exposure with your signs, bring a ladder, some large nails, and a hammer with you when you put out your signs. When you find a busy area, locate a wooden telephone pole, climb your ladder and pound your sign into the telephone pole at a 10 to 12 foot height. You are definitely going to get much longer exposure because the city workers can't just pull them out of the ground like they can with the ones with the stakes. In fact, you're probably going to piss them off a little bit. Oh well :). You're on your path to financial independence. You're an entrepreneur making moves and doing what you have to do. You're a freight train making it happen. Got me?

Now, there was one point where a police officer called me and wanted all of my info so he could send me some kind of ticket or fine. I told him I couldn't talk right then and I would call him back later. I never called him. Remember, all they have is your cell phone number and they would have to get a judge to get a subpoena to investigate your cell phone number and get your full information. It's not going to happen. He is just going to trash your sign and hope that you don't put another one out again.

There are multiple places you can find deals on bandit signs online. Just search online for real estate bandit signs and plenty of options will come up. They usually take a couple weeks so get your order in ASAP! Don't forget to order the metal stakes. I had one student that forgot to order them one time and he had to wait another week before he put out his signs. That's not cool.

One thing I want to stress here is that you do not need to be stressing out about colors and styles of the signs. Get a simple sign and order it ASAP. Details matter in certain scenarios but this kind of stuff will just slow you down if you think too hard about it. Let's move on to the next way to get sellers calling you...

Local Publications

This strategy has gotten me quite a few deals over the years. Here's the thing about this – it takes a little trial and error before you find the most effective place to put your house buying ads. I want to quickly cover the actual wording of your ad first and then we will get into where to put them.

When you create an ad (in any industry) to market yourself, you want to cover the pain points of your prospect. It's an absolute fact that humans take more action in life to avoid pain than they do to gain pleasure. So, when you word your ad, you want to focus on the problems they may be having in their life or with the house that would cause them to need to sell. Then, obviously, you can present your solution. That is "simple sales copy 101." I am, by no means, an expert on writing sales copy, but putting together a simple ad is not genius work. You know that I am an "example guy", so let me give you a simple example of an ad:

- *Are you sick of evicting tenants?*
- *Are you tired of dealing with repairs and expenses on your home?*
- *Are you done with the expenses and maintenance on that vacant home that you inherited?*

We pay CASH for houses and we don't care what the condition is.

We can close in less than 2 weeks and get that headache

property out of your name. Please call for a "no obliga-
tion" discussion about how we can make you a fair offer.

Now this was a very basic, yet effective, example that high-
lights the seller's headaches and then goes into the very clear
solutions for them. You don't want to be too wordy. People
don't have time to read a bunch of BS. You want to hit them in
their face immediately with highlighting the pain. They can immediately raise their hand and say "that's me" and then call you.
You can craft the ad with different words if you'd like, as long as
you maintain the basic structure that I showed you. Think about
when you watch those infomercials on TV. The first thing they
highlight is how painful the current way of doing things is and
then they immediately present the product that solves the pain.
It's not rocket science. It just works, and has always worked. It
presses the right psychological buttons that makes all humans
act. You are the "aspirin" to their headache. Ok, enough with
the ads. Now I'm going to talk about the places you need to
put them.

The first publication that I placed an ad in was a free book-
let/magazine that was placed in gas stations and little grocery
stores in a certain portion of the city. It was like a glorified cou-
pon/weekly deals book and there was a classified ad area in the
back. I ran into it because I had a friend who had a cousin who
was a sales rep for the publication. My friend gave him my number because he figured that I would be a good fit as a business
owner looking to market myself. He called me and asked if I
wanted to place an ad. He told me that a small basic ad in the
back of the book was $21 per week. It reached thousands of
people, so I thought I'd give it a shot since it was so cheap. I
actually got a few calls pretty quickly and got a deal my second
month running the ad. You never want to quit something just
because you didn't get a deal within the first month. These marketing tactics that I'm teaching you require consistency and it
would be a shame for you to give up right before the floodgate
of deals open up to you.

Once I realized how effective these small publications were, I immediately started to search out other ones like it in different parts of the city. I'm an obsessive freak when I run into something new that really works, so I was nonstop looking and trying all kinds of stuff. I ran ads in many other places, but as time went on, I started to narrow it down and focus on a few key places that were actually effective on a more consistent basis.

Church Bulletins

The next place that really got me decent results was church bulletins. I found a few local Catholic churches that had ads in the back of the weekly bulletins that they pass out every Sunday after church. I contacted their ad rep and negotiated the rates. I noticed that the sellers that contacted me seemed to trust me a little more and were friendlier than usual. The reason is that they hold you to a higher standard and automatically assume you have integrity and are honest because you are part of the church bulletin. This really makes it easier to gain fast rapport with the sellers (I will be teaching this very shortly) so you can move forward to the "deal making" a lot quicker. I really do love church bulletins. Some can be pretty cheap and some are more on the expensive side. I think the most expensive one that I did was $2500 for a year's worth of ads with 3 different churches. It was a package deal and I was a little hesitant at first, but I'm definitely glad that I moved forward with it. I specifically remember a deal that I rehabbed and flipped for a $65,000 profit. Not bad, right?

I am still always trying small, unique publications with mostly strikeouts. Once in a while I get a deal and it covers ALL of my strikeouts and then a whole lot more. It's worth a lot of the trial and error. Some of the publications are going to be total flops, but when you find ones that work, it will all be worth it. The nice thing is that most of them are pretty cheap and should not break the bank.

Here comes the next place for ads...

Newspaper Ads

Now, this strategy for ad placing is not as cheap as many of these smaller publications that I have talked about. I really do love newspaper ads because it is becoming less and less competitive because of all of the technology advances over the last few years. I remember when I first started, the "real estate wanted" section was filled with ads and it was really hard (and expensive) to stand out. You had to invest in extras like colors, bold print, and all other kinds of eye tricks that the newspaper had for sale. It was really frustrating. The great thing about all of the online stuff that's going on is that when you place an ad in your city's main newspapers, you won't have a ton of competition. When someone is searching the paper for someone that they can sell their house to you will pop out at them and they will call you. As much as you think that everyone only goes on craigslist these days, it's not at all the truth. In fact, the baby boomer generation and older still read the newspaper regularly and use it to find different solutions and deals that they want and need. Many of the best motivated sellers that you are going to deal with are going to be older people that are done with all of the headaches. Do NOT overlook local newspaper ads. They are a little more expensive though. In fact, in my city, the main newspaper charges around $2500 for a year of Wednesday and Sunday ads. It's not bad though if you get even one deal from it. It will pay for years of future ads. Make sense? Good. Let's move on.

Business Cards

This one is pretty much common sense, but again, most people don't think of this when they are trying to just be an "investor." I've made it crystal clear why you don't want to become an investor so I don't really need to say any more about that. You need to create simple business cards with some key information about what problems you solve and who you help. Business cards are dirt cheap online nowadays so there should be ZERO excuses for not getting them.

The information on your business card should be very similar to the wording on your publication ad that I mentioned previously. Then you can just throw in a simple graphic and you are on your way.

Remember, business cards are only good when they are in someone else's hands. What I like to do is put them up on corkboards at local businesses and grocery stores wherever I can. You can hand them to people everywhere you go and tell them that you pay referral fees for successfully closed deals. I have definitely gotten deals over the years with cards, but again, it all comes down to being consistent with getting them out there into the hands of as many people as possible, as often as possible. This is no time to be shy with strangers here. You need to be confident in your approach and tell people what you do. We are talking about creating your family's financial independence for crying out loud! Just get out there and do it.

Direct Mail (absentee, driving for dollars)

Here is where it starts to get really fun!

Now you are going to find out some of my more advanced strategies for getting consistent deals. Sending letters consistently to certain groups of people will result in a very good and consistent response.

I am going to be upfront with you right away on this topic. It is one of the most expensive ways to find motivated sellers. It's not cheap and it is something that only works with consistency. But, you have to remember that in the big picture, it's still dirt cheap when we are talking about starting your own business from scratch. Just remember that when you are thinking about how expensive some of this marketing is. The other option is to play it extremely safe and stay miserable for another decade or three. Does that sound like a better option? I didn't think so...

There is a right way and a wrong way to send mail to homeowners. I am going to explain what I have learned after wasting tens of thousands of dollars on letters and postage.

The first group that you are really going to send letters to is absentee owners. These are owners that don't live in the property. The nice thing about these leads is that they are most likely tired landlords. They really don't have any emotional attachment to the property that can make things harder to negotiate. There are a lot of reasons that these leads are ready to sell at a discount. Here are some of those reasons:

- Evicting a tenant
- Getting divorced and need to liquidate properties
- Too many city work orders
- Back taxes
- Sick of maintaining vacant property
- Liquidation of an inheritance
- Bankruptcy
- Vandalism of the property
- Etc...

Obviously these aren't the only reasons the sellers would be motivated to sell quickly and for a discount, but they are usually the most common. When you catch a seller with one of your mailings that is currently going through one of these headaches that I just mentioned, they will call you, and you may be able to close a good, profitable deal with them. Now you have to remember that just because they call you and even explain their problem to you, that doesn't always mean that they will be willing to sell at a deep discount. It's just that this list of homeowners will be more likely to be motivated. There are no guarantees with any list, but you need to start mailing to the one with the highest likelihood of someone calling you to save them from their problems.

Now, before I go into what to mail them and how often, I want to talk to you about another group of homeowners to mail to that takes a little more work, but can be extremely profitable. Remember this, the more work it takes to find certain leads, the less likely that your competitors are willing to do it, which equates to more opportunity for you.

So, this next group of people I want you to mail to comes from driving around for a while. Here's what you need to do. Drive around the money areas (I described them earlier) and write down all of the addresses that look run down and may even be vacant. By the way, if you can afford it, you can pay someone else to drive around and do this too and offer them a small commission if you close a deal. Now when you have a decent list (at least 100 addresses), you can send these people a sequence of letters. The reason they are likely to be motivated to sell quickly and for a discount is pretty obvious, isn't it? If their house is run down and vacant, it's costing them money every month to own it. They are paying utilities and taxes, cutting the lawn and shoveling snow, and other miscellaneous tasks. What if they live far from the property? It sure sounds like a headache to me. You might be asking why they wouldn't just try to sell it the conventional way with a realtor. Remember, these people know their house isn't perfect and they might be in a distressed situation that needs a quick resolution with cash. Believe me, the more you mail to people like this, they more you will see how many homeowners out there need your services.

What to Mail and How Often

Okay, now that you know who some of the most likely motivated seller leads in your area are you are going to need to know what to send them and how often. I can't stress enough that all marketing success (in any industry) is based off of consistency. You can't mail 250 letters one time and if you don't get a deal say that mailings don't work. That's absolutely insane.

What you are going to do is send the property owner an initial letter saying that you are very interested in purchasing the property quickly for cash. Again, you are going to use similar wording as you would in the ads and business cards that we talked about earlier. You do NOT want to make this extremely long and hard to read. You want to focus on a few key pain points that you are looking to solve for them and that's it.

You are going to want to hit both of the above mentioned lead lists three times before you are done. So you are going to "touch" each lead three times. You might be thinking that if they want to sell they will sell to me on the first mailing. That is absolutely not the case at all. People's circumstances can change quickly and if your message is not in front of them at the time they need you, they won't call you. Most homeowners will just toss your letter in the garbage when they don't need you. They are not thinking, "I may eventually have problems where I need to sell quickly for cash, so I'll keep his/her number." Trust me they are not thinking this at all. That's why consistent marketing is so crucial and it's why most beginners struggle and eventually throw in the towel. This business is very simplistic, but most people are just lazy. That's as blunt as it gets.

Here's an example of the power of multiple mailings to the same person:

Johnny Homeowner has owned a rental property for twenty years and things have gone pretty well with the occasional headache. You send him a letter telling him your message and he hasn't thought of selling anytime soon and just tosses it in the garbage and considers it junk mail. Now, a week or two after you send him the letter, one of his tenants loses their job and can't pay the rent. Meanwhile, you send him another letter 90 days after the first one and he has this little dilemma on his hands with this tenant. He figures the tenant will eventually get back on track so he tosses your second letter. Then, another month or two goes by and the tenant says that they haven't found a job and they still can't pay. Johnny is sick of this and he realizes that he has to evict them. He sends the tenant the five day notice and he also gets another one of your letters. Now he is faced with a decision: Does he go through with another expensive eviction or does he just get out of this thing and not deal with it anymore? Some sellers will deal with the eviction and others will call you for relief. Your first two letters were completely meaningless to him, but that last one was "gold" to him. Get it?

Getting the Absentee Owner List and Getting the Mailings Out

There are multiple places online where you can get the absentee owner list. I'm not here to promote or endorse any one in particular, but if you search online, you will be able to find lists very easily.

So once you buy the list, usually 20-30 cents per lead, you can move forward with your marketing to them. There are many different styles of letters that you should use for the different "touches." I prefer to use yellow letters on the first two touches to the targeted leads. These are handwritten letters on yellow paper with a handwritten envelope. Again, I don't promote anyone in particular, you can simply search online and you will find plenty of companies that can mail for you once you send them the list you have. So, the first and second touch should be a handwritten yellow letter, and then the third one should be a postcard. I have done all of the trial and error for you. I have tested different sequences and letters many times. I have lost tens of thousands of dollars by doing mailings that just don't work. Postcards are much cheaper than letters and it's the final shot at getting the seller's attention, so you can spend the bare minimum on the third touch.

Now, you are going to want to send these touches in 90 day increments. So, for example, if you send your first letter to Johnny Homeowner today, you are going to send out your next letter him 90 days from now. Then you are going to send the final postcard 90 days after that. This is a solid 6 month time frame to get their attention to see if they are motivated to sell. From my personal experience, I've noticed that after that 6 month time frame, I'm wasting my money by continuing to reach out to this person.

Your first letter should say that you are interested in buying their house at "ABC happy street" and describe their problems and how you can solve them in a clear and concise way (refer back to the ads). Your second letter should be a little shorter with some type of language stating that you are "still" interested in buying their house. Then the postcard will also state that you are "still" interested in buying their house. One thing that I also added as a "PS" on the end of each letter is:

"I only want to buy if you want to sell"

I will explain why that "PS" was a huge shift in my types of responses in the next section.

The 90 day time frame is the perfect sweet spot that makes the most sense after years of trial and error. I will tell you, right now up front, getting the calls is just the beginning of this process. From there you will have them in your phone call funnel. Again, I'll explain this in the upcoming sections what I mean by that.

I really want to teach the nitty-gritty details here that some of the other education courses out there seem to skim over or overlook completely. These small details are crucial and add up to one big result in the end, which is BIG PROFITS consistently for you. Make sure to join the email list over at AlphaHome-Flipping.com where I share even more unique tactics that no one else is using.

Dealing with all of the Different types of calls

I want to let you know that there will be a variety of calls that will come in and some of them may really surprise or even shock you. Actually the type of call can be very different depending on the type of marketing that got them to you.

When sellers call you, you are going to want to get some key info from them as quickly and conversationally as you can. You don't want to sound scripted, but in the beginning it's a little tough not to. That's okay and totally normal. Don't obsess over it. You will be talking to thousands of sellers throughout your career in this business and your first few will not go as well as you will like. That's how I started, along with every other savvy entrepreneur out there. You will hang up and be mad at yourself for what you said or asked. You'll wish you would have said "this" or "that". I really don't want you to lose any sleep over that stuff because you will naturally get better in a very short amount of time. You don't have to try very hard, it will just happen. Consistency is key (notice a theme here about consistency?).

Do you remember the "PS" at the end of the letter that I just mentioned? After years of tweaking my letters, I realized that it weeds out a lot of leads that would call and be mad at you for bothering them to sell their house. It lets them know that they should only contact you if you want to sell. Now, back to dealing with seller calls...

You will need to get some key info from the seller that will determine how you will proceed with the call and if you will end up meeting them or not. The better you get, the less time you will need to decipher the quality of the lead.

Here are some key questions you will want to ask:

1. What's the address of the property you'd like to sell?

2. How long have you owned it?

3. Is this your residence or a rental property?

4. Why are you selling?

5. How soon would you like to sell?

I just want to interrupt this list for a second to point out that I am not initially asking them how much they want, how much work it needs, etc. These initial questions are for understanding their psychology and motivation. These factors will outweigh all of the "numbers stuff" and allow you to either move further into the call or to realize that this won't go anywhere and you will be wasting your time. Now, in the beginning, I want you to talk to more sellers than usual to get your feet wet and get comfortable talking to sellers. Most of your success in this business will revolve around dealing with sellers the right way.

I will get to the questions you need to ask after the ones listed above are answered, but I want to break these down further so you can fully understand how this initial part of the conversation should go and how to respond to different answers to these questions.

When sellers say that they have owned the property for a long time it means that they, most likely, will have a good amount of equity in the property. You need there to be equity to make your flips profitable.

If they tell you that it is a rental property there is a different psychology in play. They will not have an emotional attachment to the property and selling it will be strictly a business decision. They don't have to worry about moving their personal stuff or where they are going to go once the house is sold. It can happen pretty quickly and smoothly. A lot of times this will allow you to make a better deal in a much faster amount of time. They just want the thing off of their hands for one reason or another. It is probably just a headache for them and they are done dealing with it.

If they tell you that it is their primary residence the conversation will go a little differently. You will ask them if they will rent or buy after they move. You will ask them how soon they want to move. I have even paid for their moving truck if it is a roadblock from closing the deal sooner (obviously the profit will have to be worth doing it). They will have to let go of years of memories so they may need some time to think about it and this could make things draw out a little longer than you would like. Remember though, you need to realize that this house is really about them and solving their problems and that's how you will make nice profits. If you go into these conversations like a greedy pig trying to push them to close tomorrow, you won't make it very long and sellers will send you on your happy way before you'll even have a chance to negotiate a good deal. Don't be a selfish schmuck that is only thinking about yourself; you'll kill your business before you even start.

Now, the magic question:

"Why are you selling?"

The reason I call it the magic question is because it's probably the most important question you will ask. It's extremely important because it will ultimately determine the level of motivation of the seller. Remember, high motivation is the key here. This is where you will let them talk and don't interrupt. You want them to go deep if they want to. I have had people come up with all kinds of reasons about why they are selling. Some of them have been really off the wall. The point is that the more painful the reason the more negotiating power you will have. You are not taking advantage of these people, you are solving a problem. Any successful business makes a profit because it solves a problem for people. This business is no different.

If people say things like "I'm selling because I just finished remodeling the entire house and I'm ready to get top dollar for my house", you're not going to be making a deal with them. If they say things like, "I saw your ad and thought I'd give you a call because anything's for sale at the right price", they are just fishing around and not really motivated at all. These will not turn into profitable deals. But remember, in the beginning, I want you to be talking to these sellers more than usual because

I need you extremely comfortable talking to sellers as soon as possible.

The next question is about how soon they would like to sell. This is also a great indicator of their level of motivation. If they say that they want to sell as soon as possible, that means that they are ready to make a deal right away. When they say things like, "I'm in no hurry", or "I'm just starting to put feelers out there to see how much I can get", they aren't that motivated and you shouldn't waste too much time with them. In fact, I pretty much laid out how to decode all of the answers of these initial questions to determine if they are worth pursuing further. Once you have determined that they are motivated, you want to ask them a few more key questions before you actually set up an appointment to go and meet them.

The next group of questions you are going to want to ask are:

1. Does the property need any work/updating/remodeling/repairs?

2. How old is the roof, furnace, kitchen, bath, etc.?

3. Have you researched roughly how much homes around you are selling for in a similar condition?

4. Do you have any idea what a fair price would be for your house?

This next round of questions should be all you need to talk about before determining if you are going to go meet them and look at the property. When you ask them what kind of work the property needs and they start listing different things; that is a good thing. The repairs and remodeling are the things that are going to allow you to get a discount from the retail price of the home.

If they answer with something like, "the house doesn't need anything and is in perfect shape", the likelihood of you getting a bargain on this house is pretty low. This is not 100% fact but just keep it in mind as you continue talking to the seller.

The next question dives a little deeper into the condition of the property where you find out if there is some deferred maintenance that will need attention soon. If these items are near the end of their lifespans you'll have some more negotiating power.

When you ask if they have done any research on values and if they have any idea what a fair price would be, there can be a wide range of responses. They may say things like, "yeah, the guy next door just sold his for X." Or they might say, "I have no idea." They might respond and say they want you to just make them an offer.

If they come up with some kind of "fair price", I always like to ask how they came up with that figure. You'd be surprised at some of the answers. Again, you really just want to get into their mindset of how they are thinking so you can understand where they are coming from and create a win/win deal that can benefit both of you. Regardless of what price they come up with, you still can get a great deal. Many times it's strictly a starting point and doesn't mean a whole lot. I once talked to a lady who told me she wanted $90,000 for the property over the phone and I ended up meeting her, looking at it, and buying it for $16,000. I really got to understand her needs and where she was coming from and how much pain the property was causing. There were drug dealers in the property and were not cooperating with her at all. I showed her some of the surrounding values, explained how much work needed to be done, and we made a deal. She walked away from that closing table with a smile on her face.

After you have gone through these questions and have seen some responses that indicate motivation, you will tell the seller that you would like to meet them and look at the property. You can say that hopefully you can make a fair cash offer on the property after you see it.

Hounding Sellers

There is one important thing that I want to go over with you here before we talk about meeting with the seller. You are going to get calls where people want to sell, but for some reason, you can't totally get an appointment set up because they aren't quite ready for one reason or another. They may even say that they will call you back and let you know when the time comes. They will NOT call you back no matter what. People have so much going on in their lives and don't have time to remember you or how you can help them. They live their lives moment to moment and if they are ready to sell they will pursue whatever avenue presents itself at that time that has the least resistance. So what you need to do is "hound" sellers after their initial phone call.

There is a saying that I heard a long time ago that says, "The fortune is in the follow up." This applies to all sales and persuasion scenarios, and this is no different. The first call is always the defensive "no thanks" and from there it can get better and more open. You have to stay in front of these people constantly so when their circumstances even change slightly, you're right there to make a deal. I can't stress enough that they will not go look up your phone number in their neatly organized rolodex and give you a call. I promise. Call them once a month, at least. It will pay you in volumes. That, I also promise.

The winners in this game aren't afraid to hound people to make a deal. I can't tell you how many times I have had sellers get extremely annoyed and sick of hearing from me, but in the end, make a deal with them because I was the guy that stayed in touch. There was one particular deal I remember where this lady owned a property that I really wanted to buy. We could not agree on a price and she also wasn't quite ready to sell. I called her every single month for a year and a half. She was annoyed a lot of the time, but in the end she was happy with the deal. I came up a little on my price and she came down because of how persistent I was. Persistence does really pay in this business and it accounts for almost ALL of the profits I have made. Eventually you will get to an appointment with the seller and be able to make a profitable offer. Sometimes it just might take a while.

Chapter 5

Strategies and psychologies for gaining rapport and dealing with sellers

You've asked all of the right questions over the phone, determined the seller's level of motivation, and made an appointment to look at the house. Great job. You're moving right along this very simple process. Did you notice how I didn't say "easy process?" There's a difference between simple and easy. The entire process of putting together a profitable real estate deal is, conceptually, very simple. Moving through each step and getting to a closing table is not easy though. If it was super easy, everyone would be doing it. I will say that the more experience you gain over time, the easier each deal will get. There will always be those headache deals, but going through the process will become second nature. The good news for you is that if you are consistent and persistent, all the right doors will eventually open. That's a promise.

Subchapter – Meeting with the seller at the property

Meeting with the seller requires some finesse and strategy and I'm going to go over everything that you're going to need to know that is involved with the encounter. First of all, never park in the driveway. Always park on the street, it's the respectful thing to do. It basically says that you respect their property and you realize that those spots may be for other people that they are expecting. If this is an absentee owner, he or she may take advantage of their time down there by meeting you, another buyer, a realtor, a family member, or anyone for that matter. Being on the street is the way to go.

Once you walk up, make sure to have a sincere friendly smile on your face, shake their hand, and say, "hi, I'm Nick, thanks for meeting me here today." This initial situation will show them that you are respectful and very friendly. This will go miles in your rapport building and your negotiation. No matter what, you really want the seller to like you. You may think that it doesn't matter and it's all houses and numbers but guess what, this is a people business whether you like it or not. If you hate people, stop reading right now and never even think about getting into the real estate business. It's true.

Okay, after that quick rant I'm ready to move on.

After the initial encounter you also want to quickly ask if they mind if you take photos of the property. You can simply tell them that it's much more effective than writing a bunch of notes on a clipboard of the condition and it takes a lot less time. Usually they won't mind. These photos will definitely come in handy when you are estimating repair costs later and obviously you will be forwarding these photos to your buyers so they can qualify the deals to see if it's something they want. The more photos you take the better. The more you can show your buyer before he or she walks through, the more likely you will close the deal because they've already seen the photos and it looks like a property that they will want to buy. They are simply walking through to verify what they've seen in your photos.

As you walk through the property you want to consistently be gaining more and more rapport with your seller. You want to be very pleasant and conversational and continue to find out more and more about their situation and their problems with the property. All of these details will reveal their true motivation and intentions. See, sometimes the seller will have a guard up and say things that they don't really mean. They may say that they need to get top dollar for the property, but when you listen to them talking about how fast they need to sell to settle a divorce, the truth is revealed. You have to remember that the more rapport you build with the seller, the more they will let their guard down and trust you, which will let them open up to you so you can make the best deal possible to solve their issues. If you always have the "problem solving" mindset first, the profitable deals will come.

After you walk through the property and get all of your photos, you will thank the seller and tell them that you will get back to them as soon as possible with an offer. You will be making offers on every property that you look at, but most of them will not be accepted. You are going to have to get used to making a lot of offers and getting rejected on the majority of them. If all of your offers are getting accepted, that means you are paying way too much. You do not need to write an actual offer (contract to purchase) until a verbal price is agreed upon. It's not worth your time to write an offer until an agreement is made.

Subchapter – Coming up with an offer price

I'm sure you're asking how to come up with an offer price. Well, it's not nearly as hard as you think and you don't need to be a genius with a ton of experience. Even though there are no exact formulas in this business, this is a pretty accurate rough formula that has served me very well over the years (I will explain all of the terms below):

ARV x .70 (or .65 for a little negotiation breathing room) = variable A

Variable A – repair costs = variable B

Variable B – your desired wholesale fee = the price you want to pay.

Ok, let me break this formula down so you can make sense of it. First we need to talk about ARV. This stands for "After Repair Value." This is what the house is worth when it's completely fixed up and ready to be put on the market for a retail buyer. There are multiple websites out there like Zillow.com, Trulia. com, or Realtor.com that have all the information you need to find the ARV of the property you are looking at. You will search for the property and then find all of the recent sales around that property that are similar in size, bedrooms, baths, etc. and see what they sold for. Look at the photos to make sure that all of them were nice and retail ready houses. Obviously there will be some oddball prices in there that are houses that were in rough shape similar to yours. You also want to get a good feel of the price per square foot for the fixed up houses in the surrounding area so you can calculate that for the property you are looking at. Once you figure out the ARV you are ready to move further through the formula. You will take the ARV and multiply it by .70 or .65 and you will arrive at a figure. Then you are going to take that figure and subtract the estimated repair costs for the property.

Figuring out repair costs for the property is also a figure that is pretty easy to come up with, even if you don't have any extensive construction experience. Again, nothing is carved in stone, but this formula is a pretty good rule of thumb that you're going to want to implement. The typical cosmetic rehab (kitchen, bath, flooring, paint, windows, and light fixtures) usually costs between $30-$35 per square foot. If it needs a roof, siding, foundation work, furnace, or anything more major, you will have to add those things in. Lighter rehabs that just need some paint and carpet and some minor stuff usually ranges around $12-$18 per square foot. These are rough estimates to get you out there making offers. You will refine this more and more as you progress and get a tighter feel on exactly what a lot of these things cost, but this is a simple way to start.

So once you subtract the repair costs from the prior number you end up with variable B. Now it's simple. You subtract your desired wholesale profit from this number and that becomes the price you will want to pay. You will usually want to offer a few thousand less, so that you have a little room to negotiate. I learn really well by examples and I'm sure you do too, so I'm going to show you one:

You are looking at a house that has an ARV of $140,000 and you want to know what to offer the seller.

$140,000 x .65 = $91,000

Now you know that the house is a full cosmetic rehab that is about 1,200 square feet.

$91,000 – $42,000 = $49,000 (the $42,000 figure came from 1200 square feet x 35)

I really want to make $7500 on this deal.

$49,000 – $7500 = $41,500 (the price I want to pay).

Now, it's never always cut and dry. I told you, each deal is unique and there will have to be a little "flexing" in all of this, but these are great starting points and safe strategies to work off of in the beginning, especially. I have a few other articles about making offers over at AlphaHomeFlipping.com.

When you make these offers to your seller I want you to arm yourself with some powerful ammo. These offers, many times, may shock the seller or make them laugh at you because it's way too low. I told you before, that's why you need to always be looking at a lot of deals, because most of your offers are going to be rejected. The powerful facts that you will be presenting to your seller are as follows:

1. You can pay cash.

2. You buy in "as is" condition.

3. You don't bring in a home inspector.

4. They don't have to pay thousands in real estate commissions.

You will call your seller and tell them that you have come up with a figure that you are prepared to offer them. By the way, you never want to take longer than 24 hours to call your seller back and make an offer. Truly motivated sellers really appreciate speed and you don't want to disappoint them by making them wait. You will remind them of the four facts that I listed above before you give them a number. Then you tell them what you want to pay. Remember, their first reaction might be pretty surprised.

Now, when you make them the offer, a few different things will happen.

The first situation will be where they are just so motivated to sell that they accept and then you can move forward to writing a contract to purchase.

The second situation is where they will laugh and say that there is no way in hell that they will sell for anywhere near that price and they will feel completely insulted. That's not a problem. Don't freak out if they get a little defensive and go on the attack a little. You simply thank them for their time and you move on. I really want to stress that many of your offer calls are going to go south quickly and that it's part of the process. It's business. Don't let your emotions get involved. I know how anxious you are to get a deal going, but this whole business is nothing more than a numbers game. What I mean by "numbers game" is that the more sellers you talk to and more offers you make the more profitable deals you are going to do.

The next situation that can happen when you make your offer is your seller being slightly offended and also confused on how you came up with the number. They may even ask you how you came up with that offer price. It's okay if they ask that. You can even be transparent and explain to them the repair costs. You can also tell them about other miscellaneous costs like a real estate commission when it's sold(after buying and fixing it up), holding costs, utility costs, small profit for doing the deal, etc. (that .65 − .70 number we talked about earlier). That .65

– .70 figure that you are using is for your rehabber to make a profit and cover those miscellaneous costs I just listed. You can explain all of this to them and you can also tell them about the real addresses of sold properties that you used to find the ARV. This is plenty of authentic and verifiable ammo that the seller can't deny. I even go into telling them that "my opinion" of value doesn't matter. I tell them that I speak strictly off of raw public data so there is no dispute. I explain that I am transparent and I can show them any of this info that they need to see. When they hear you say this, it shows your honesty and transparency and allows them to even trust you further. You may need to email or send them some of this stuff so they can see it all for themselves. Sometimes they will take your word for it since you've told them that you can easily show it to them if they want.

Another situation that may come up is that they say they have to talk to one or more other parties who are part of the decision making process for the house. It could be a spouse, sibling, attorney, etc. Whatever it is, you have to respect that and realize that they need a little time. What you need to get out of them before you hang up the phone is when they are going to make a decision. I literally ask, "What day do you want to have this decision made by?" When they tell you a date, make sure to call them on that day and ask what they came up with. I never depend on anyone to call me back.

The last main situation that will come out of your verbal offer to the seller is that they will immediately fire off a higher number and try to negotiate with you. Now, you decided on your wholesale profit when you made your offer, so you may have to shrink it a little if you really want to get the deal. Also, the nice thing about my offer formula is that the numbers allow for slight breathing room to where you can still wholesale the deal for a profit, even though you flex inside those numbers a tad. It's not ideal, but you can still make money if you bend the formula a little. The nice thing is that, in the next section, I will teach you how to write your contract to purchase in a way where you can legally walk away if you don't find a buyer to come and get your wholesale payday.

Subchapter – Moving into the purchase contract

This is the beginning of the real action that it takes to get your physical paycheck. Let's get moving...

When you actually come to a verbal agreement with your seller, you will want to move forward and write an offer. Some states call it an "offer to purchase" or a "contract to purchase." Strategically, I use the standard blank offers that you can get from your local legal blank or office supply store. A lot of people think that they should have their attorney draw up some custom offer that fully protects them. I purposely don't and here's why:

1. I usually meet with the seller and fill in the blanks of the offer with the seller. I also tell them, "This is the standard offer form from the local legal blank store." I use it instead of a custom offer because there is no special language that would favor me, the buyer. I also use these forms so we can go through and fill it out together so you can stop and ask any questions along the way. This goes back to the foundational principle involving the seller's guard being let down, trusting you, and feeling extremely secure dealing with you.

2. I also use these forms because there are still areas where you can insert custom language to make the seller feel really safe and secure with your offer. I will explain this language in a second.

Okay, so now that you know what kind of contracts to use, let's talk about getting in front of the seller to write it. The first thing you want to say when you guys agree on a price is that you'd love to meet and put together the paperwork to make this deal official. You can meet at the property, coffee shop, or wherever. The bottom line is that you want to get this thing locked up in writing as soon as possible because the seller is fully on board with the deal. Don't push this meeting out for a week or even days. Try to meet within 24 hours or less while the verbal agreement is extremely fresh.

Now I'll go over the different responses that will come out of you saying that you want to meet ASAP to put it in writing. By the way, many sellers freak out when you tell them you want to put it in writing, even when the price and terms are verbally agreed upon. The fact that the paperwork makes it totally real can slightly engage somewhat of a small defensive psychology in the seller again. It's not something that happens all the time, but it can, and will happen to you throughout your years in this business. It's okay if this happens. They may say that they want an attorney to go over the paperwork before they sign anything. That is totally fine and you don't want to try and talk them out of it because that will initiate even more of a defensive mindset because they will wonder why you would try and talk them out of it. Just simply answer, "okay, I am flexible and work with attorneys all the time and would not have a problem working with your attorney." From there, they will decide if they still want to have an attorney review the contract or maybe they just wanted some type of excuse for not signing it on the spot. The bottom line is that if they insist on not signing on the spot and want to wait, you must honor it without any hesitation that might alarm them.

The other response they may have, and the best one, is that they are ready to meet ASAP and sign the offer with you. Again, set up the appointment to meet within 24 hours, and seal the deal.

The most ideal scenario is for them to move forward immediately to the offer signing, but if it doesn't work that way, don't get upset. Most likely you will always still get the deal because I'm going to show you what to write in your offers to make them really "clean." What I mean by "clean" is that there is nothing weird or lopsided with things massively in your favor and not protecting the seller in any way. The goal is to make the seller (or their attorney) feel as protected as possible in the contract. This is extremely easy to do and I'm going to explain it to you now.

I'm going to go over the key areas of the offer that you will want to address.

The first part is going to be where you are going to put the general information about the parties involved and the property address. Some contracts need your name as the buyer and some need the seller name as well. You will then input the property address.

The next area you will address and fill in is the earnest money. Earnest money is the amount of money that you will give to the seller to, kind of, "confirm" the deal. You need to make it a small amount like $10 or something. Many states require some form of earnest money to make the contract fully valid and iron clad. From there you will want to go over the items inside the property (appliances, light fixtures, furniture, etc.). I always write that "seller's personal property is not included in the purchase price." This leaves it open ended where they can take what they want, and leave the rest. It sticks with the theme of protecting the seller.

The next part of the offer that you will want to address is the contingency areas. A contingency is, basically, a clause that allows the terms of the deal to change if the result of the action (inspection, appraisal, financing) isn't satisfactory to the buyer (you). The more contingencies, the more the deal favors the buyer and you don't want that. If the seller thinks that the offer is weighing too far in your favor with all of these different "outs", then they will feel that the offer is less appealing. NOT GOOD! An example of a contingency would be an inspection contingency. This is where you would hire a home inspector to walk through the property once the offer is accepted. From there, you could look at the inspection report and go back to the seller to make them change the price, do some work to the house, or you could walk away altogether if you wanted. You are buying the house in "as is" condition and that's why the seller called you, so this is NOT something that you will be using. Somewhere on your offer there will be a few blank lines where you can write some custom language.

Here's the magic language that will make your seller love you and protect them at the same time:

"Buyer is buying property in "as is" condition with no warranties. This is a cash offer without any home inspection or financing contingencies. This offer is only contingent on my partner's approval."

These phrases protect the seller from warrantying the condition, which is definitely something that separates you from the average conventional buyer out there. They will also love that it is a cash offer without the usual "out clauses" from conventional buyers. The last sentence is your only "out" and it is key. Your partner will be your cash buyer that you are going to flip it to. If they ask how long it will take your partner to approve it, tell them it usually takes 2 weeks or less. They might ask why you need your partner's approval and you can tell them that they are the ones that come up with the cash most of the time and you are more of the deal finder. You just want to assure them that you will make all of this go as seamless as possible. Remember, truly motivated sellers don't push too hard with this kind of stuff, because they just want to get rid of the house. If they keep trying to back you into a corner simply tell them that you are trying to put a fair deal together and this is how we do things (respectfully, of course).

You are also going to set up a closing date and place, which you will extend out 30 days if possible. This will give you enough time to line up your buyer and get the deal set up for a "smooth sail" closing. You will make the designated closing place your title company that you set up early on. Everything else on the offer should be general info about the deal.

Now once your seller has signed the offer, you each take a copy and you are ready to make the moves that will get you your profit.

Chapter 6

GETTING PAID...Bringing your Buyers Through the Property

When I first started off wholesaling properties, I understood a lot of it, but I always wondered how the heck I was supposed to show my buyers the property when I didn't even own it. It was a concern of mine and over the years, through trial and error, I have refined many ways that can work. Keep in mind, every situation is different in this business, and that's why you will always need multiple strategies in your arsenal so you can find one that you can easily plug into certain scenarios. The strategies I'm going to talk about have to do with how you will present a "pre-closing walkthrough" to your seller. You want to make sure that you present this the right way so that you don't end up with them rejecting the idea completely.

The most ideal scenario is for the seller to give you a copy of the keys. Obviously, this will only work out if the property is vacant. Even then, the seller may be hesitant. You want to say something like, "If you don't mind, I would like a copy of the keys so I can run my partner through as soon as possible so we can close right away." You can also mention that you like to plan out the exact work that needs to be done so you can get rolling right after closing. I want to be very up front with you and let you know that you getting the keys won't happen that often. Most of the time the seller will say that they will want to meet you at the property to let you in. That's totally okay. In fact, the majority of my wholesale deals were done this way. If you do get a copy of the key you are golden and can obviously set up showings with your buyers whenever it is convenient for you. If you don't get the keys, keep reading this section.

If the seller insists on meeting you down at the property, no problem. Now you just have to make a few more phone calls in order to set up the showing. Just ask them something like,

> "I'd like to run my partner through the property as soon as possible and maybe some contractors. If I call and set something up a day or two in advance can you please meet me down just to let them in? It won't take more than 15 or 20 minutes. We will be really fast.

Most of the time, they will happily agree to it. They are motivated, remember? This makes all this kind of stuff become super seamless and easy. Once they agree to this, you are golden.

Let's recap...

You will tell sellers that you want to walk your partner through and have your contractors inspect the property. You can mention just the partner thing, or you can mention both right away. Feel it out and if the seller's guard is down and they are open to you, just ask them the simple question and move forward. Don't be afraid to ask. You'd actually be surprised how much motivated sellers will agree to. In fact, I did a deal once where the house I was looking at was in extremely rough shape, to the point that I almost passed on it altogether, because I really didn't think it was worth anything. I know that sounds nuts, but I thought it was worthless. But, before I chalked it off completely, I knew of one of my buyers that likes to buy houses over in that area and thought of an idea. Before I even wrote an offer to the seller, I told them something along the lines of this,

> "Hello seller, the house is in extreme disrepair and I really don't think it has much value at all. There is a small

chance that I might be able to help you out though. If you could give me a copy of the keys so I can really get in there and figure out the nitty gritty numbers, I could possibly get you guys out of this so you could move on."

They were so motivated, that they actually agreed to this **before I even wrote them an offer!**

That's the epitome of dealing with a truly motivated seller. I brought in that buyer I was telling you about and told him I needed $19,000 for the house. He said the absolute best he could do was $10,000. I told him I would get back to him in a day to let him know if I could make that work. When I left my buyer, I immediately called my seller and said I could do $2,500 for the house. They quickly agreed. Before I even wrote my seller an offer, I called my buyer and told him to write me the offer for $10,000 right away. He wrote it the same day and then I quickly sent my offer of $2,500 to my seller and it was all signed and locked up. We closed 2 weeks later and I pocketed over $7,000 for a deal that I almost passed on. In fact, I chronicled this exact deal on video over at AlphaHomeFlipping.com.

You will want to maximize the time your seller is willing to meet you down at the property. Make sure you tell a few of your buyers about the deal and show it to them at the same time. This creates a more competitive environment which forces them to give you their highest possible offer if they want the property.

Your next question might be, "Nick, how do I keep my seller away from my buyers so they don't expose the price of my signed agreement?" Good question. Again, after years of experience, I use something that is so simple. All you do is have your seller open up the house, and then let your buyers walk through while you have small talk with your seller near the front of the house or wherever. Just isolate the seller where you can have a very friendly conversation that draws attention away from your buyers walking through the house inspecting. It's not genius, by any means, but it simply works. Then, when the buyers are done, tell them you will call them soon and send them on their way. After they all leave, tell your seller thanks, and tell them you'll be in touch soon. Done!

Subchapter – Locking up Your Buyer with a Profitable Contract

Now, later on, you will be talking to your seller over the phone. If you brought a few buyers through at the same time then usually the buyer will call you sooner than later because they know that they are in a competitive scenario. Great news for you!

When you talk to the buyer, you want to let them know that you have other cash buyers interested and that they should make you the best offer possible. I am assuming that you already told them the initial price that you were asking (your wholesale markup). If you approach it with the "best offer" language, you may end up getting more than you originally asked. I have been in that situation many times and it's a great place to be. I'm a huge fan of always remaining in the driver's seat and portraying to all parties that you are offering something extremely valuable that they want, whether it's a buyer OR a seller.

As soon as you verbally agree on a price with one of your buyers, you will tell them to write a contract to purchase. Try to meet them as soon as possible to just get it done. Once they do, there are a few ways you can structure this deal (we talked about the different types of transactions much earlier on).

The first way that you can do this deal is to structure a simultaneous/double close. Remember, this transaction is where the seller and you have your own closing statement, and then you and your buyer have your own closing statement. There are a few small costs in doing it this way, but it's very clean and easy. Your buyer's funds will blanket the whole transaction and you will pocket the difference, minus title and closing fees.

The other way you can structure the deal is with an assignment of contract. The first thing you're going to want to do is make sure that your buyer and you have both signed his contract to purchase the property from you. You will then fill out a simple, one page assignment of contract, which will spell out the assignment. The form will also name the assignment fee, and that is why I have them write the contract first, so they are committed to the price, even after they find out how much your assignment fee is. Again, most savvy buyers don't care what you're making because they know they are getting it at a great price that works for them. Once you fill out this form and you each have a signed copy, you're ready for the next step...

Forwarding the Paperwork to the Title Company

This part is extremely easy and you're pretty much home free. You have all of your contracts signed and ready to go. You are either ready for a double close or an assignment closing. You will fax or email these documents to your title company and let them know to get working on the title work and closing paperwork as soon as possible. They will contact you, your buyer, and your seller soon after that so they can get the basic info they need to get the deal done. I'm talking about things like address, phone, any lien waivers, etc. Nothing complicated. Since the title company you are working with is very familiar with these types of transactions, you really shouldn't have to tell them much. They will just know what to do to get the deal closed smoothly and quickly.

Staying in Touch with All Parties between Contract and Closing

This is something that I take very seriously. I am in frequent contact with my title company to make sure that everything is going smoothly. This can be as simple as a quick email asking if there are any issues or if there is any information they need from any party to speed things up. You don't want to be obnoxious about it, but you do want to stay on top of it.

I also make sure I'm in touch with my sellers. Remember, they aren't familiar with the process of selling houses, so they still might be a little nervous. You will simply call them a few times prior to closing to let them know that the title company will be calling them soon to get some basic info. You can also re-assure them that everything is running smoothly and the closing should be very quick and efficient. You have to remember that life situations can change rapidly, and you want to be on top of your seller's mindset in case something changes with them. I've had deals where the seller went out of town and talked to their relatives and they told them that they were selling the house for way too cheap (of course they are experts on out of town property values, lol). When I called them, they had a different tone in their voice and I had to slowly get them back to reality. The point here is that if I didn't stay in close touch with them, they might have let this crazy info they got from their ignorant relatives grow into something bigger in their mind and tell me at the last minute that they wanted to walk away from the deal. It has happened to me before in the early days and I don't want it to happen to you. Nip negativity immediately and you will be rewarded long term.

As far as my buyers go, I stay in contact with them once or twice too. Once you get a better and stronger relationship with them you don't need to bother them as much, but in the beginning few deals you want to make sure that they are ready to perform with their cash. Usually, the buyers don't cause much of a problem and are savvy on how the whole transactional process works.

I don't want you to downplay this very important point. You need to take it very seriously, because if you don't, it could end up costing you tens of thousands of dollars. In fact, every little detail in this book is extremely important, even if it sounds like no big deal. I've learned many valuable (and costly) lessons by brushing over little details. Don't fall into the same lazy trap. Many of the small details covered in this book are over-looked completely in the entire real estate education industry as a whole, and that's why I'm trying to cover all of them here.

Subchapter – Getting to the Closing Table

Okay, so once you get everything to the title company and you have been in touch with your buyer and seller, the closing is what happens next. This is where you get your payday. The first time you close on a deal it is going to feel like a life changing moment for you. You are going to realize that you just opened the door to a whole new world of income and opportunity for true freedom.

When you get to the closing, your buyer will be in one room and your seller will be set up in another. Most of the time you can be in either room or you can opt to be in your own room. I usually go with the seller first to make sure everything is going smoothly for them and then I will quickly bounce over to my buyer's room just to verify that everything is good there too. Everything usually is good because the title company knows exactly what they're doing and how to make this flow smoothly for you. That's what they get paid to do. The forms will be signed by both parties and within 30-60 minutes, the whole thing will be done. The title agent will hand you your check and you can leave and start looking for your next deal.

Before you leave, you will definitely want to thank the sellers for being so cooperative and making everything so easy. Even if they didn't do anything, always thank them and make them feel good. The last thing you will do is ask them if everything went as smooth and simply as you originally said that it would, and if they say yes, kindly ask them if they could write a short testimonial for you. These can be very powerful when you show them to future sellers. It gives you very solid social proof and le-gitimacy. When they say ok, tell them to make it simple and just to describe how easy and fairly everything went while working with you. It will pay volumes for your future business. Don't take this detail lightly.

As far as talking to your buyer, you will simply thank them and also ask them how soon they will be ready for another one. Remember, you have other buyers, but the difference now is that you know FOR A FACT that this one can close easily with cash and no headaches. That is extremely valuable. In fact, I've made a few thousand less on some deals just because I know that my buyer can close. I could've called some of my other buyers and tried to get more, but betting on a sure thing is the path of least resistance. Once you get going at this, you are only going to be dealing with a handful of your buyers list because you will realize that getting paid from them is a matter of one phone call. That's going to get you freedom very quickly. You don't always have to show it to 10 people to try and squeak out every last nickel out of these deals, you just want a steady flow of paydays so you can get to the next level.

Chapter 7

Why I am not focusing on you 'making millions'

I want to touch on something that I find very important involving learning how to do this business right. Most of the educational material available about flipping involves a lot of hype and statements like:

"Make $30,000 in 30 days with my secret system"

"Become a Real Estate Millionaire"

"Buy 50 houses a Year with No Money"

"Wake up and flip houses from home in your underwear"

Etc....

Let me explain something to you...

This is all hype. I'm the biggest optimist that you will ever meet and I truly believe that anyone can accomplish anything they want in life. I will, however, say that extreme results take super extreme action. It takes action like you may have never seen or experienced before. The point is that most of the big headlines written in this education industry are created to get you to buy or click onto the next page for more sales pitches. I'm also a capitalist that believes in a free market and the fact that anyone can market and sell anything they want. I'm not even really knocking these guys that are out there marketing the hype. What I am knocking is the ignorance of the people that think there is an "easy button" for this business. There isn't. Real Estate is the greatest business in the world and probably one of the oldest. It has been around for, literally, thousands of years.

The point I'm trying to make here is that you have to do your own homework and due diligence when you are learning (in any industry), and then you have to go out and take the action necessary to get the results. So many people jump from hyped up course/program/secret system or whatever to the next boot camp/seminar/secret system and they never end up taking any real action to get their first deal done. And by the way, if you've ever gotten sucked into any of these hyped up things you will realize that there are many farfetched strategies that will never get you to an actual closing table.

I didn't start off this book and write it with the goal of showing you how to make millions and retire in one year. Is it possible? Absolutely. Is it realistic for most people? No. The absolute purpose of this book is to navigate you, from start to finish, through your first profitable deal. If you can get through it with a nice profit you just opened a beautiful door that WILL get you to financial independence if you can rinse and repeat your first deal. If you can do one, you can do one hundred. Now that's not hype, that's a simple fact. If I started off by saying, "if you read this book, you can become financially independent in one year," you probably would've thought, "yeah, maybe, but not me." I'm not saying that though. I'm saying that all I want you to do from this book is to get just one profitable deal under your belt and you will be more on your way to something greater than you've ever seen.

Do you want to know the real secret to being a successful real estate entrepreneur? Here it is:

THERE IS NO SECRET OR SECRET SYSTEMS!

It's just taking simple steps, and over time getting better and better at them with experience. The nice thing about this business compared to most others is that the financial barrier to entry is extremely low, and you really don't need any experience. Most other businesses you start, you need to get loans, create a product or service that you hope and pray that people will want and buy, or you're out of business and belly up. You don't need to create anything here. Real estate already exists, you just need to know how to navigate it right and work it to your advantage. That's all folks. You don't need to push anything down anyone's throat or sell your brains out to someone who doesn't want your product or service in the first place. I don't know about you, but I feel that this business definitely is the path of least resistance in the entrepreneurial world for sure.

When I say that this book will get you to do your first simple and profitable deal, it sounds very attainable to where you will actually try. Big promises usually cause people to not even try because it sounds too big and they are not used to doing big things in their usual daily routine. I'm trying to break your usual routine in a subtle and very attainable way. You are not building Rome in a day, week, or month. You are building your personal Rome over a relatively short period of time that actually makes sense. Your results will definitely come if you approach this business one deal at a time until you are ready to expand. Remember, you are starting a REAL business and it takes effort. Luckily this business is based more on effort than start-up capital. That's obviously another very attractive trait that makes this one of the greatest businesses in the world.

Millions can come if you keep pushing with maximum effort, but I'm not here to sell you on some get-rich-quick millions junk. DO YOUR FIRST PROFITABLE DEAL! I really can't stress this enough.

Remember, you are about to be an entrepreneur. We talked about this label earlier, but I really want to make sure you fully understand what it means. Some of the key traits to being an entrepreneur are:

1. Super Persistence.

2. Not caring what others think about what you're doing.

3. Ready to Learn in ALL situations.

4. Ready to Adapt in ALL situations.

5. Willing to make sacrifices in the beginning that will pay them for life.

6. Being Extremely Decisive.

7. Being able to gain rapport with people.

There are other traits, but these are a few key ones that you really need to focus on and embrace quickly. Some of these traits won't come overnight, but they are all learnable and able to be attained over time. Success in this business from complete scratch absolutely requires that you adopt the traits of entrepreneurship. You MUST be an entrepreneur. If you had a few hundred thousand to throw at something to get a return, I would be having a completely different conversation with you and you probably wouldn't be reading this far into the book. This book was written for you, the person that is ready to come from the ground up and put your stake in the ground. It's for the person who finally wants to create something for their family and have the freedom they know they deserve. There is an open sea of opportunity in this business all over the world.

My story, along with many others, completely crushes your excuse barriers. It really doesn't matter what your starting point is because I came from zero once, and from bankruptcy a second time. It's all about consistent action. You should be visualizing your new life every day that you wake up and every day when you go to sleep. This will keep some fuel in the tank that you will need, especially on some of those tough days where you feel like throwing in the towel. Let me tell you, I still have those days once in a while where I get extremely fed up, but my dream is way too big to get trumped by some stupid problem or issue that will eventually go away. Yours should be too. Really take the time to vividly imagine how your life could be if you could do just a few extra profitable deals per year. What would it look like? What would that mean for your family? What would that mean for your kids? What kinds of freedoms would you be able to have? The sky is truly the limit, but trying to take on the world in 30 days is very unrealistic. Get one deal done; then move on to the next. Get it?

If you've read this far, you should realize that you have a real deal blueprint in front of you. You realize what it takes to get a profitable deal done. There is no reason why you can't start TOMORROW. I'm very serious about this. Don't put this book down and think about it. Don't go around asking the opinions of people who are not financially independent if it's the right move for you. They don't know JACK! In fact, people who are not financially independent will absolutely tell you not to do it. They know that if you rise, it will make them feel like they are falling. Nobody wants to feel like they are falling. That's extremely uncomfortable and they will tell you to "play it safe" and not to do it because then everything in your friendship/relationship will stay the same. Staying the same is safe. Guess what...Playing it safe is the new "risky." Do you follow? I really hope so.

I NEED you to take massive action starting tomorrow. Use this book as a utility to refer back to and really get moving. I can't stress this enough. I run into people all the time that spend so much time learning, they don't ever take any real action. Learning doesn't get actual results, action does. I don't care what you're trying to pursue. Most people know the simplistic ways to make changes in their life, they just don't do it. It is crazy, but we all fall into this trap here and there. Tomorrow could be the first day of the rest of your life, or it could be another boring chapter in the long book of monotony. The fork in the road is waiting for your decision. There's that word "decision." Does it ring a bell? Remember the entrepreneurship traits? Yes you do!

After hearing my crazy story, and the inspiration from it, you really should realize that you are no different than me. I wasn't born with anything special. I'm a regular dude with a huge drive in me. PERIOD! You and I are no different and I can't stress that enough. I just realized that there really are two ways to live your life:

1. You can live off the script that someone else writes.

Or

2. You can live based off of the script that you write.

Make your decision. Deciding is all there is to it.

I was broke and bankrupt. If you are too, I proved you can do it.

I wasn't born with special people skills. I developed them with conscious practice because I knew it was necessary for entrepreneurial survival. You can too.

I've wholesaled plenty of deals without a dime of my own money, you can too.

You and I are the same. We are human beings that are trying to create the greatest, happiest, and most free life that we can on earth. It's okay that some people start off in life rounding third base. It's okay that you are only a batboy/girl. Comparing yourself to others will surely make you miserable. That's an absolute promise.

Once you do your first deal, the sky is truly the limit and eventually you will get into rehabbing and selling these same deals for even larger profits. You will be paying cash for rental properties that will pay you for the rest of your life if you want to. You can do whatever you want or don't want. Maybe you'll just wholesale properties forever. I teach these other things too, but again, I'm trying to just get your foot in the door with a nice profit on one solid first deal.

One thing I can tell you for sure – I've been on both extremes of the wealth/financial spectrum. When you're financially independent, life can be much easier, happier, and more fulfilling. Money does NOT create happiness, but being financially independent will take away one of the number one stresses that most families deal with every single day. That can be a start to happiness. I hope you agree :-)

It's been an absolute pleasure talking to you about my story, some inspiration, and all of the tactical steps that you will need to get you to where you want to be. I hope that this book is the single item that finally pushes you over the edge to take that first step. Remember, I believe that real estate entrepreneurship is the best way for the average person to gain financial independence. I really do believe it and I think I made a pretty darn good case for that throughout this book. I also believe that you should follow your true passion. Real estate entrepreneurship may be the foundation that will allow you to branch out and blossom to bigger and greater things, which you have planned in your life that may have never been possible, without the financial rewards of flipping some deals.

Remember, all of this comes down to one thing – DECIDING!

23998758R00060

Made in the USA
Middletown, DE
10 September 2015